The Cats of Britain

An Ideal Gift for Cat Lovers With Lots of Great British Cat Stories and Fun Trivia (a Funny Cat Book Featuring Shakespeare, Beatrix Potter, Churchill, and Cat-Crazy British Millionaires)

Seamus Mullarkey

D11103681

The Cats of Britain: An Ideal Gift for Cat Lovers With Lots of Great British Cat Stories and Fun Trivia (a Funny Cat Book Featuring Shakespeare, Beatrix Potter, Churchill, and Cat-Crazy British Millionaires)

Table of Contents

1- SPECIAL BONUS!

Want This Bonus Book for FREE?

Get <u>FREE</u>, unlimited access to it and all of my new books

SCAN THE CODE OR CLICK THE LINK...

subscribepage.io/h6Fz5k

2- Acknowledgments

Thanks to everyone who encouraged me in this endeavor. It took far longer than I thought, and I'm so glad so many people have said it was worth the wait. Thanks to one and all of you!

3 - Preface

"If it be true that nations have the cats they deserve, then the English people deserve well in cats, for there are none so prosperous or so friendly in the world."

—Hilaire Belloc, from "A Conversation with a Cat"

4 - Dedication

To the magnificent British moggies in all their glory, who populate both town and country, from Land's End to John O' Groats...

Cats have witnessed much during their time in Britain, being present at many historical events such as the building of Londinium by the Romans in the 1st century, the Norman invasion of 1066, and the devastation of the Great Fire of London in 1666. During waves of the Black Plague, superstitions against cats—associated with witches and others close to the devil—were bad news for the poor pussycats. Still, it was finally determined that the destruction of cats brought more bad luck. Without their fearsome rodent hunting skills, the flea and rat populations increased. Apart from their valuable abilities, they had cuddly countenances, and appreciation for the felines grew.

Today, British cats enjoy a place at the pinnacle of the pet hierarchy—there are more than ten million pampered pussycats in Britain—not to mention they hold a ubiquitous position in British popular culture. You can find cat lore in folk tales, in historical monuments, in entertainment, and in the hearts and minds of many illustrious Brits as well as throughout the institutions that the British hold dear.

From nursery rhymes to service during wartime, cats occupy a unique place in British culture and history. One of the longest-running musicals in theater history is the estimable *Cats* by Sir Andrew Lloyd Webber. I hope that you will find much to marvel at in this little tome about the magnificent cats of Britain. Please note that as this book was initially published in the US, both the spelling and punctuation follow American conventions.

Above all, this book is a highly personal (and incomplete) assessment and history of the cats of Britain. I know there is so much more to say on the subject, and there are most definitely things I've overlooked. I'm not an expert on history or cats, but, like many of you, I'm an eager gatherer (and relater) of historical trivia and odd snippets of information. So, bear with me and browse this compendium of cat stories, conveying what cats have meant to Britain and what an important place they will continue to occupy in British hearts and minds.

I hope you enjoy reading this book as much as I enjoyed writing it.

JUDGING IN THE RING AT THE CRYSTAL PALACE.

1871, The First National Cat Show at the Crystal Palace

Nanny Knows Best!

Before the 1700s, a nanny and a housemaid in well-to-do homes were often the same role, meaning that the nanny would take care of the children while cleaning the house. However, the term "nanny" came to describe a different concept from the 1700s onwards. The culture of the nursery and its attitude towards animals would come to shape the British upper classes for hundreds of years. The warning "Nanny knows best" was the rule of law.

7

Nannies might indeed be strict, but they also added fun to the lives of their charges. Nanny routinely recited nursery rhymes to entertain *and* to convey moral truths. These poems often featured animals, which brings us to the topic of cats and how they were used to teach valuable life lessons. For example, "Hickory Dickory Dock" focused on a clock that had a small hole where a resident cat lived and hunted mice, hopefully instilling the values of patience and hard work in children.

While the British in the 19th century still adhered to the biblical imperative that Man ruled over the animals and could do what he pleased with them, there was a growing awareness that the cruel treatment of animals was concurrent with or led to cruelty towards humans. Thus, nannies took pains to instil tenderness towards animals in young British hearts.

Perhaps the most direct guidance on avoiding cruelty and practicing kindness toward kitties is the British nursery rhyme "Ding Dong Bell," which dates its origins at least back as far as the 17th century. Although there are many variations, it tells us "pussy's in the well," asks "who put her in," and then shames the little bully who dunked her and praises the junior hero who pulled her out. It goes on to declare: "What a naughty boy was that, To try to drown poor pussy cat, Who ne'er did him any harm, But killed all the mice in the farmer's barn...."

Grown men and women routinely kept in touch with their nannies and, when visiting their childhood homes as adults, would pop up to have tea with Nanny in the nursery before even thinking about seeing their parents.

One of the most famous nannies in British history was Winston Churchill's nanny, Elizabeth Anne Everest. She was with him from birth until he was seven years old. As Churchill himself wrote, "She taught me how to walk, to talk, to eat with a fork, and above all to be a good boy...It was to her that I poured out my many troubles." Maybe it was she who inculcated in him his lifelong love of cats?

There's Always Time for Tea

One of the most recognized spoils of the empire, tea, might not have been a catalyst for the conquest of India, but it was undoubtedly one of the perks. You can see why cats would swoon at the mention of teatime. This delightful occasion is when the porcelain jugs of milk and cream or morsels of meat just ripe for the swiping go on irresistible display. Tea, it must be emphasized, is so central to British culture that there is no modern way of understanding the Brits without their teatime ritual. It was initially popularised in the 17th century by King Charles II and his Portuguese wife.

Initially ridiculously expensive and kept under lock and key, tea was a luxury reserved for the upper classes. This situation changed late in the Victorian era when the working classes took tea—with hearty meats and snacks—right after work, as they didn't usually get a lunch break. This "high tea" is not to be confused with "afternoon tea," which is a more sumptuous spread of dainty delicacies like crustless sandwiches and small cakes.

The origins of afternoon tea can be traced back to 1840, when Anna, the 7th Duchess of Bedford, started to experience a mid-afternoon lull in energy. Maybe she ought to have taken a cat nap? In any case, she began requesting tea, sandwiches, and pastries from her servants in the late afternoon. Gradually guests were invited. The popularity of afternoon tea soon spread throughout society, with particular emphasis on the presentation and quality of the food and drink.

While today the Brits drink tea at any time of the day—the ceremony of teatime doesn't quite fit into current schedules. Yet, although the elaborate rituals surrounding teatime might not have the same cultural relevance in the fast-paced contemporary world, tea still represents comfort and coziness for many inhabitants of the Sceptered Isle—much like a snoozing cat curled up in one's lap.

Many British workplaces still have 15-minute tea breaks (usually one around 11 am and one, later, about 3 pm. These are a chance for colleagues to gossip over a "cuppa" and claim they'll go on a diet next week while tucking into a sugary biscuit (cookie to our American friends) or three...

Gardens: Nature Purr-fected

The British have always loved their patches of green and the art of gardening. Whether taking a stroll on the lawn or having afternoon tea outside (in between the rain showers!), traditional British houses are inconceivable without a planted plot of some form. From the simple cottager's mixtures of flowers and vegetables to the intricate parterres of the manor house, it seems there's a garden for everyone. Gardening programs regularly top the television ratings, and their presenters are well-loved national celebrities.

The history of English gardens can be traced back to as far as the Romans. These featured symmetrical hedges and gravel walks. There were mazes that provided kittens and cats the purr-fect place to play or nap uninterrupted. During the medieval period, monasteries planted herb beds both for culinary and medicinal uses. Catnip (or catmint as it was known then) was cultivated by the monks for use by humans. It was said to either calm humans or make them more aggressive – as with cats, the reaction to catnip depended on the individual. Some made use of the plant as a gentle sedative, while it's said that hangmen (who were presumably among those whom the herb rendered aggressive) made a tea of catmint to rev themselves up before hanging poor unfortunates on the gallows!

More modern British gardens draw heavily on the influence of the inimitable Gertrude Jekyll, who in the early 20th century delighted the British with brilliant colors and a more exuberant style. Apart from gardening, one of Jekyll's passions was making sketches of her cats. These feline portraits became the cornerstone for an important chapter entitled "Pussies in the Garden" in her much-loved title, "Children and Gardens."

Apart from private gardens, many British have enjoyed gardening in allotments. These are more extensive tracts of land acquired by local municipalities and then sub-divided into plots that residents can rent and cultivate.

These public gardening spaces were made possible by the Allotments Act of 1887 and were designed to provide fresh vegetables for the poorer classes. Over time, they also became social spaces where proprietors of neighboring plots could chat about their crops and whatever else the other conversational topics of the day might be.

Unfortunately, in more recent years, the conversation on the Walsall Road Allotments in Birmingham took a concerned tone when news spread that the allotments were in danger of being bulldozed to provide space for the sporting facilities that would host the Commonwealth Games.

Thankfully, the plans were eventually shelved. The allotments were saved with the help of a Twitter campaign featuring none other than Robert the Allotment Cat, one of the community of feral cats who peacefully co-existed with the gardeners on the allotments. On "his" Twitter posts, Robert, a handsome cat of midnight black hue, successfully appealed to gardeners and cat-lovers across the country to sign a petition to help save his home. We're so glad the gardeners and the kitties at the allotment will get to enjoy their delightful green oasis for years to come!

It would seem that cats are even willing to risk one of their nine lives for the privilege of attending a garden show. Back in the early 2000s, adventurous kittens Smokey and Dotty ended up in the undercarriage of a truck carrying nursery plants to the Chelsea Flower Show. The cats presumably thought the underneath of the vehicle was an intriguing and safe place to explore. While they must have been terrified on the sixty-mile journey, they stayed put—not even jumping off at traffic lights. They were finally discovered by their owner, Rosy Hardy, when the vehicle came to its final stop at the world-renowned garden show. We hope it was worth it for the intrepid kitties and that they enjoyed the show!

From those with an allotment to those with an extensive spread, or even just a geranium on a windowsill, gardening is culturally ingrained in the Brits. And cats have left their paw prints in those gardens. Many British cats tend to be indoor-outdoor cats and get free access to "their" gardens.

Acknowledging cats' predatory nature, a substantial number of British moggies get a bell on their collars to thus warn the songbirds that are attracted to gardens.

So, if you hear the delicate tinkling of a diminutive bell while in an English garden, it's not Tinkerbell coming back from Never-never land. It probably indicates that kitty is doing the daily rounds of his domain. Just like British humans, our furry brethren find that there's much to admire and enjoy in Britain's lovely, lovely gardens.

Not Making a Show of Oneself

Humans have an inherent desire to show off their possessions and accomplishments. However, the somewhat reticent British generally prefer not to make overly ostentatious displays. However, exceptions are made for certain occasions, usually featuring plants and livestock as well as home-baked goods and yummy pots of jam at county fairs or village fetes across the country. At these events, a certain amount of competitive display and just a hint of boastfulness are tolerated.

History records the very first cat show in 1598 at a fair in the English town of Winchester. It resembled a sideshow and featured cats who were lavished with prizes, hailing them as the best ratters and mousers in town. No one cared a whit for the featured cats' slenderness of limb or whether the tip of their noses had an aesthetically pleasing tilt. The cats displayed were beasts of utility, not to be considered from an aesthetic standpoint or for representing the purity of characteristics from a particular breeding lineage.

Fast forward to 1871, to the Crystal Palace exhibition hall, an architectural masterpiece that boasted 23 hectares of ground space. This massive glass structure was the impressive venue for a historical feline event. It was there that, on July 13, 1871, the first modern cat show in the world was held. The organizer of the show and first president of The English National Cat Club, Harrison Weir, was distressed by the fact that cats, as domestic animals, were often persecuted, ill-treated, or simply misunderstood. He bravely decided that "it would be well to hold 'Cat Shows,' so that the different breeds, colors, markings, etc., might be more carefully attended to, and the domestic cat, sitting in front of the fire, would then possess a beauty and an attractiveness to its owner unobserved and unknown because uncultivated heretofore." We're sure that cats across Britain appreciated that they were now being considered in the proper light.

Finally, they had ascended to the heights of the British class system and were at last becoming *aristo-cats*.

Fiercely competitive, the first cat show boasted 170 entries and displayed many curiosities, including a cat with 28 claws! The second national cat show at The Crystal Palace in December of the same year had triple the number of entries. Cats were clearly tightening their grips on the hearts of the nation! Weir passed away in 1906, firmly entrenched as the "Father of Cat Fancy." His 1889 book *Our Cats and All About Them* is considered one of the early classics on the subject. Harrison Weir, we—and our cats—salute you! You were a British gentleman of the finest sort...

See You in The Pub!

Short for "public houses," pubs are a central part of British life. They truly are a home away from home for many Brits. Some of the finest urban examples (with ample stained glass, shining brass, elaborate wood carving, and etched mirrors) date from the 19th century when they were dubbed "gin palaces," where the poor could take refuge from their dreary accommodations for the price of a drink. Meanwhile, in towns and villages across Britain, a different style of pub expresses its rural roots through welcoming fireplaces, timbered beams, and cozy country style. These social spots were often initially coaching inns, where those taking horse-drawn coaches on longer journeys could refuel with food and drink. Travelers would stay the night, and then (with their rested horses having had a chance to regain their strength), be on their way once again.

It probably won't surprise you to know that felines play their part in the pub culture of Britain. Many pubs have used cat images on their signs. This trend began around 1393 when Richard II commanded that pubs and inns needed to exhibit signs with images (not just words), as most people could not read at that time. These colorful, intriguing, old-fashioned signs are still fondly displayed throughout the length and breadth of the United Kingdom and enliven the landscape with their thought-provoking names and images.

"The Cat and Fiddle" is a rather popular pub sign, used in at least a dozen British inns and pubs. It is not a tribute to a cat's talent with a particular stringed instrument but was supposedly named after an English knight whose name in French was *Caton Le Fidele*, or "Caton the loyal." This name sounded like 'cat and fiddle,' so that's the image that was displayed. Other pub signs borrowed from noble coats of arms, attempting to use lions and leopards as their models. However, most regional painters had never seen such exotic animals, so they used the familiar domestic cat as their muse. There was also a well-known inn in Essex called "Just the Cats." The moniker makes perfect sense. Cats, as we know, are great lickers, and in the pub, people get great liquors! There is a British pub called "The Cat With No Tail" in -guess where?- the Isle of Man, homeplace of the great tailless wonder of the cat world, the Manx cat.

Cats, of course, make excellent pub companions, purr-fectly happy to keep you company as you sup. They can also conquer any countertop as well as they can capture even the hardest of hard-working hearts. A pub in Bristol, The Bag of Nails, once boasted 24 resident cats, all born in the pub. However, that number was eventually whittled down to 15 as some were taken to lucky homes. The remaining pride are currently all competing for prime lap space from the many willing customers.

6- SOME VERY BRITISH CONCEPTS

University, The Dreaming Spires

The British university has been the model for institutions of learning worldwide. Facsimiles of its quadrangles and castle-like buildings crop up on campuses everywhere. Cambridge and Oxford are undoubtedly the two most famous universities in Britain. Founded back in medieval times, students there have long been able to enjoy feline company while they study

Sam the cat, for instance, has enjoyed a free run in New Hall at Cambridge University—except during the spring when the little ducklings in the college pond start to hatch. Generally, this kitty can be found curled up in a comfortable office chair or sunbathing on the walkways. He is the pampered prince of the university, fed by everyone from porters to students. It is said that, if you get on the right side of this finicky feline, your university years will be showered with awards. His primary function is to help members of the Cambridge University Cat Club get over their loneliness at leaving their felines at home. This high-brow kitty also feels at ease in a relatively rarefied environment. As Mary Archer so aptly put it in *Cambridge Cats*, "no animal...so unconditionally slavish as a dog could feel at home in the academic courts of Cambridge, but cats—watchful, self-contained, in-scrutable cats—are their natural companions."

Sam and Cambridge are only one example among many of the collegiate cats on university campuses in Britain. There have been Molly and Dorothy at Oxford. Recently, Dennis the cat at the University of Buckingham developed a loyal following on social media, even earning enough to pay his vet bills.

Loyal to the Royal Mail

Founded as a government department in 1516, the Post Office in Britain has played a crucial role in British society. Its Penny Black, issued in 1840, was the world's first adhesive stamp and made sending letters accessible to far more people. For the first time, the sender paid the cost of sending the letter rather than the recipient. Business boomed and the British Post Office was overwhelmed with letters. These high heaps of mail (along with parcels containing food-stuffs) provided an ideal breeding ground for vermin. Initially, poison and traps were used to keep the bothersome rodents at bay. However, in 1868, it was decided that cats would be hired for the job after noxious poisons and mechanical traps were deemed dangerous for postal employees. Not everyone was thrilled about this development, however. Some resentful workers complained that fetching and carrying cat food was an inconvenience and an embarrassment – welcome to our world. However, most of us cat lovers would consider that "burden" a privilege.

One shilling per week was allotted for the care of the cats at the beginning of their tenure. A century later, this stipend had only risen to ten shillings. In fact, in 1952, public outrage was expressed because the fiscally efficient felines hadn't gotten a raise in many years. This public clamour might have mainly been due to the enormously popular Tibs the Post Office Cat, whose outstanding record at keeping the Post Office Headquarters vermin free garnered much attention in the popular press. Tibs served a tenure of 14 years in the 50s and 60s. By the 1980s, the cats were granted an allowance of about two pounds a week. It is estimated that, at one point, 25,000 or so cats were employed by the Post Office. The last cat employed at the Post Office headquarters went by the name of Blackie, who passed away in 1984. No new cats were taken on as the Post Office had replaced cloth mail sacks with sturdy, rodent-resistant plastic sacks.

Kindness for All: The RSPCA

The founding of a society for preventing cruelty to animals was a long time in the making. In the 19th century, with the rise of the middle class and steadily increasing living standards, domestic pets became a more feasible addition to the household. Accompanying those evolving attitudes toward animals came a desire to protect the welfare of various animals used for labor (draught horses, for example) as well as those embraced by families as beloved pets.

In 1824, Reverend Arthur Broome and Richard Martin (nicknamed "Humanity Dick"), among others, met to establish a society that would pressure Parliament to enforce statutes that would forbid "wanton cruelty" to animals. This was a tall task, as in the those days the lives of animals not pampered by the royals or kept safely indoors by their middle-class owners were subject to widespread neglect and mistreatment.

Finally, in 1840, Queen Victoria bestowed the privilege of using the term "Royal" in the society's title, putting her regal weight behind the society's endeavours. As mentioned elsewhere, she herself insisted on a cat being engraved on the society's medal. In the 1860s, an American by the name of Henry Bergh visited the president of the RSPCA, the Earl of Harrowby, and transported those ideas back to the United States, where he founded the SPCA. Thus, the legacy of Victorian England, with its beloved pets and conscientious aristocrats, still reverberates throughout the Western world today.

7 - Upper-Crust Kitties

Looking down on hoi paw-loi...

The term aristocracy comes from an ancient Greek term meaning "the rule of the best," set apart from what those same Greeks would have dubbed "the many," or *hoi polloi*. In our more egalitarian times, we probably find the notion of a hereditary aristocracy preposterous. After all, it only takes the accident of birth to become a lifelong member. Still, with its quirky characters and illustrious history, the British aristocracy cannot help but fascinate.

There are still about 600 aristocratic families cavorting throughout the U.K. We suspect that many of them welcome the presence of pampered pussies on their grounds and in their houses. The following are some "tails" of famous aristocrats in British history who have had memorable encounters with some rather remarkable felines.

Saucers of Cream on The Lawn

Born into an ordinary middle-class family as Louisa Catherine Ridley in 1846, Lady Marcus Beresford, as she eventually came to be, was somewhat of a sensation. She was renowned both for her affairs and divorces as well as for the elaborate care she took of her pampered kitties. The Roanoke Times of January 4th, 1889, describes the scene at Lady Beresford's country residence near Windsor where she kept 200 cats. "Every afternoon three footmen bring trays of saucers and set them out on the lawn... and every cat feeds in its own special place." Lady Beresford was an enthusiastic organizer of the first Cat Club show in 1899.

This fancy feline exhibition attracted a highly aristocratic crowd, as one can gather from a newspaper report of the time. This article noted the attendance of Lily, Duchess of Marlborough, Edith, Duchess of Wellington, Lord and Lady Marcus Beresford, Isabella, Countess Home, Viscountess Maitland, Viscountess Esher, Lady Ridley, Lady de Trafford,

26

Lady Lister, Lady Gooch, Lord Walter Gordon-Lennox, and Sir Alfred Bateman. Phew, that's a lot of titled tabby enthusiasts!

The lodgings of Lady Beresford's cats were as aristocratic as one might expect, with detailed press accounts telling of how her pets lived: "No expense has been spared in the fittings of the rooms...One room is set apart for the girl who ... feeds the pussies...On the wall is a list of the names and a full description of all the inmates of the catteries, and a set of rules to be observed by both the cats and their attendants." Lady Beresford commented about the cats' dietary requirements: "For some time, I have kept a goat on the premises, the milk from which is given to the delicate or younger kittens."

However, Lady Beresford's aristocratic feline utopia was not to last. After a period of intensive involvement with the high-society cat-breeding community, Lady Beresford eventually found the whole affair (dare we say it) too "catty.". In 1904 she withdrew from the whole social whirl of snobbish cat aficionados, commenting to the London Daily News that she was only going to keep two Siamese and a Silver Persian as "cat fanciers in general only seek profit and notoriety, and not the welfare of puss, whose cause I have so much at heart."

The Flying Duchess of Bedford

She was born Mary du Caurroy Tribe in 1865 and is ultimately most famous as a pioneering lady aviator. This trailblazing cat lady spent her early years among the British colonists in India. There she enjoyed unchaperoned riding expeditions and a few affairs before she met the younger son of a duke at a grand party in India's Government House.

Mary wasn't too enthralled with the stuffy rituals of the aristocratic social whirl. She had a thirst for adventure in the form of mountain climbing, remote yacht trips, and solo canoe trips far away from the world of tiaras and elegant gowns.

In her later years, the reluctant aristocrat became an enthusiastic aviator, dubbed the Flying Duchess for her inter-continental flights. She was devoted to several worthy causes, including hospitals for wounded soldiers and the welfare of cats. She was a highly active president of the National Cat Club. Her favorite Siamese cat (she was a prominent early breeder), Goblin, became something of a press celebrity. Newspaper articles gushed about his "glossy coat" of "cream and mouse-brown colour" and his eyes of "pale-blue mauve."

The Cheltenham Looker-On in 1904 declared, "The Duchess of Bedford has perhaps the finest collection of cats in the kingdom...her special baskets made for the favourites when travelling from one of the several homes of the Duchess to another, or to cat shows, are models of comfort and convenience." She advocated widely for more humane treatment of stray cats through impassioned speeches and founded a shelter for street cats.

The Duchess went missing in 1937 while flying in poor weather conditions over the marshy areas of East Anglia. It is assumed that she crashed into the sea and her body was never found. We're sure cats the length of the kingdom shed some silent tears for the daring duchess who adored cats and aerial adventures with equal enthusiasm.

The Royal Family's Splendid Cats

The British Royal family is undoubtedly the most widely known monarchy in the world. If you simply refer to "the

Queen" in conversation, most people will immediately assume that you are talking about Queen Elizabeth II, the current British monarch, who has had the longest reign in British history.

The British Royal Family is both subject to reverential tributes and the target of lurid, scandal-seeking press coverage. Nonetheless, the British monarchy have weathered many storms and still endured, despite the "tom-cat" antics of some of their members.

The Windsors have had quite a few connections with kitties down through the years, and cats have not been shy about being in the presence of royalty. As John Heywood recorded in his 1546 book of proverbs, "a cat may look at a king," implying that cats are not intimidated by rank and see themselves as any mere human's equal, or indeed as their superior!

There are numerous *tails* (a-hem) about the royal family's interactions with cats. From the time of the Tudors to the modern age, cats have insinuated themselves into the royal lives and residences.

Just over an hour outside London, Windsor Castle is one of

the present Queen Elizabeth's favorite residences. Her Majesty is reportedly allergic to cats and has not been seen much in their company. However, a set of drawings and doodles she made as a three-year-old, which were among the possessions of the former Royal Photographer Marcus Adams, and were auctioned in 2017, show unmistakable cat faces. These artistic artifacts are presumably evidence of an early affection for kitties.

Indeed, the Queen's historic palace has had a few connections to our feline friends down through the years. The Royal Collection Trust contains a rather intriguing ink drawing from around 1910 called "The White Cats of Windsor Castle." This is a framed illustrated poem about a white cat ghost who haunts Windsor Castle in the form of Henry VIII's various wives. Well, I never!

More recent, distinctly non-ghostly feline apparitions have been reported at Windsor Castle. One such cat made his way into British press reports in 2007. This particular kitty was named Mime and was the pet of the proprietor of a Chinese restaurant near the castle. Well, this cat seems to have a taste for the high life and made a habit of walking through the Castle gates, where she would wander in to share the food of the Queens' corgis. The guards are pretty used to her presence and happily allow this cat commoner to dine with the royal canines.

In the 19th century, Queen Victoria and her children were notable cat lovers, and she actively encouraged the royal princes and princesses to have cats as pets. Queen Victoria herself had many cats and particularly loved her last one, who was named White Heather. This kitty was described as a white, fluffy handsome Persian or Angora cat.

Victoria's son, who became King Edward VII upon her death in 1901, owned many Manx cats throughout his life and was a breeder of these no-tailed kitties. The royal collection of artworks contains a Fabergé cat ornament that Edward commissioned in 1907, perhaps as a gift for his wife, Queen Alexandra. This Danish-born royal has a special place of honor in the royal array of cat lovers. Not only did she surrounds herself with feline company at home, she also took her cats with her on royal visits abroad.

Alexandra's cats had free reign of the royal palaces. The Queen's most special feline friend was Sandy, a handsome Persian named for his birthplace of Sandringham House.

This cat had the unique privilege of being allowed in the royal dining room, although no record survives of whether he was ever seated at the royal table.

Queen Alexandra's cat entourage reportedly numbered 50 at one stage, for whom she cared devotedly. For example, any sick cats were carefully cared for in a "cat hospital," a specially equipped room attached to the royal stables at Buckingham Palace. The kitties' diet comprised mainly fish and milk, with the latter coming directly from the royal cows at Sandringham. There was no talk of milk from a humble grocery for those royal moggies!

The queen's love for her cats was immortalized in several carefully posed photographs, a great honor and a considerable expense at a time when photography required an appointment with a photographer rather than a click on one's phone. The queen also recorded her kitties' beauty in several portraits she commissioned from the renowned cat artist Louis Wain.

In more recent times, Princess Diana, the late, much-loved Princess of Wales, was known as the People's princess because of her empathetic and compassionate approach to the public. She did notable humanitarian work during her short life and remains one of the most famous royal icons. Diana had a great love for animals and had many pets throughout her life. Among these was a ginger cat named Marmalade that she had adopted as a child.

Prince Edward, the Queen's youngest son, has an interesting clothing quirk related to kitties. As the posh magazine *Town & Country* reported in 2018, the prince has been spotted wearing cat-themed ties on numerous important occasions (including at his own wedding).

We're not sure what the back story to these cat ties is. Believe us, we did some extensive investigation and couldn't find any further information., but we think it's a charming sartorial choice. Speaking of feline influences on significant royal occasions, we were amused to hear of an incident in 1998 when a stray cat wandered in to join the royal Christmas festivities at Sandringham House. The staff decided to call the kitty Queenie. Naturally, what else would she be called? They took care of her until she could be placed in a shelter. We find it quite fascinating that Queenie joined the royals just for the lavish Christmas feast, avoiding the tedious royal ceremonies and grueling scrutiny by the press that occur during the rest of the year.

These days, dogs take supremacy within the extended royal family. However, Princess Michael, wife of the Queen's first cousin, Prince Michael of Kent, who took her husband Michael's title upon marriage, is one prominent exception.

Apparently, Princess Michael's family nickname is "The Cat," and her private email address has a feline twist, which we're not at liberty to disclose. During her late teens, the princess spent time at her father's farm in Africa, where she became inseparable from an orphaned cheetah cub, who eventually ended up sleeping on her bed for a while!

Lest we think that Princess Michael doesn't care as much about more normally-sized pussy-cats, she sat for an official photograph with her Siamese cat on the occasion of her 70th birthday—and not just any old photograph. The princess wore a pink silk dress with a tiara perched atop her head, clearly indicating her royal status. Perhaps, you should get all dressed up in such a grand manner the next time you and your kitty pose for a selfie! Why let British royals have all the fun?

We should also note that, while not aristocracy in the

strictest sense, the inhabitants of 10 Downing Street—the official residence of the Prime Minister—have among them a Chief Mouser. Currently, the title is held by Larry, a ten-year-old tabby with a lovely white belly.

As the official government page explains, "Larry spends his days greeting guests to the house, inspecting security defences and testing antique furniture for napping quality. His day-to-day responsibilities also include contemplating a solution to the mouse occupancy of the house. Larry says this is still 'in tactical planning stage.'"

The Prime Minister also travels to the Palace just about every week to have an audience with the Queen: maybe Larry the cat passes along messages for the P.M. to relay to the Queen's corgis? In any case, it's lovely to think so...

The Cats of 10 Downing Street

The residence and office of British prime ministers since the 18th century, this distinctive building with its black brickwork and black front door is the venue for many important functions and an important place for foreign dignitaries to visit.

In addition to the current first cat, Larry, there have been some other memorable feline members of the prime minister's household. For example, the famed Humphrey served under three Prime Ministers, starting with Margaret Thatcher in 1989, through John Major's term, and into the long-running service of Tony Blair.

During John Major's time as Prime Minister at 10 Downing Street, Humphrey was responsible for the deaths of several songbirds; Major defended the kitty-cat's honor by stating that "it is quite certain that Humphrey is not a serial killer." When Humphrey passed away in 2006, Tony Blair honored his memory by announcing his passing to the nation as if he were a dignitary—well, indeed, he was, as most cats believe themselves to be.

One of the more famous occupants of 10 Downing Street, Winston Churchill, was, despite his moniker as "the British bulldog," a fervent cat lover. He kept several cats of his own, among them Tango, Nelson, and Mickey. During the second world war, Nelson (named after famed British Admiral Horatio Nelson) could often be found by Churchill's side, helping him to plot the defeat of fascism in World War II.

Churchill wasn't shy about displaying his high regard for cats. His private secretary Sir John Colville recalled one lunch in 1941 when the politician was considering the best military strategy to pursue in the Middle East: "while he brooded on these matters, he kept up a running conversation with the cat, cleaning its eyes with his napkin, offering it mutton and expressing regret that it could not have cream in war-time!"

Perhaps Churchill's favorite among his feline companions was a marmalade kitty named Jock, who shared his bed in his final few years. Churchill bequeathed his home at Chartwell house to the nation in his will. In memory of the special bond between the statesman and his ginger pal, Churchill's family requested that there should always be an orange cat with "a white bib and four white socks" kept in residence at the historic dwelling. This request has been honored, and Jock VII was welcomed to Chartwell in May of 2020.

Sir Henry's Cat Who Cared

Even back in the 15th century, there were stirring tales of the interactions between cats and the aristocracy. Sir Henry

Wyatt was a supporter of the up-and-coming Tudor family (which would establish a long dynasty, not to mention founding the Church of England). Sir Henry's support of the Tudors placed him in opposition to the notorious Richard III, the last of the Plantagenets. Because of Sir Henry's pro-Tudor stance, King Richard had him imprisoned in the Tower of London, where he suffered torture and deprivation to the point of starvation.

One day, when Sir Henry had relinquished all hope, praying instead for death, a cat found her way into the Tower. She seemed to know that the aristocrat needed kindness. She brought him a cooked pigeon, either pilfered from the kitchen or given secretly by a friendly guard, which staved off the nobleman's slow starvation.

The kitty continued to bring food, becoming known as "Sir Henry's caterer." The beleaguered aristocrat was eventually released after Henry Tudor became King Henry VII in 1485. In Maidstone, Kent, an inscription in the church reads, "To the memory of Sir Henry Wyatt ...who was imprisoned and tortured in the Tower...then fed and preserved by a cat."

7 - UPPER-CRUST KITTIES

Puss, The Loyal Cellmate

Another harrowing *tail* of imprisonment and feline redemption comes from the Elizabethan period. The third Earl of Southampton, patron of William Shakespeare, was also imprisoned in the infamous Tower of London. The Earl had been involved in the Essex rebellion and was first sentenced to death before being sent to the Tower.

This fearsome fortress was guarded by ferocious cats in the form of lions in the moat, members of the Queen's official royal menagerie. However, legend has it that security was breached by a cat of a far more diminutive stature, an ordinary housecat called Trixie, who was most devoted to the imprisoned Earl. She would pitter-pat across London to make her way to his cell.

In reality, Trixie the cat might have been brought to the jail by the Earl's wife. However Trixie got there, the kitty stayed with the prisoner to comfort him throughout his gloomy incarceration. There is actually a portrait of the earl that dates from the time of his imprisonment featuring a black-and-white cat crouching next to him as if on guard.

The nobleman was released after James I ascended the

throne upon Elizabeth's death. We're sure that the earl spent a good deal of his new freedom frolicking and sharing treats with his little feline chum, who had cheered him up during his gloomy prison stay.

"Downton Tabby"

One of the most beloved portrayals of the heyday of the British upper classes of recent years has to be the TV hit, *Downton Abbey*. Fans of the aristocratic soap opera who are cat lovers will be delighted to know (if they haven't heard of it already) that a highly creative writer has come up with a *purr-fect* parody, full of feline intrigue and hairball-raising drama.

The book *Downton Tabby*, written by Chris Kelly, tells the *tail* of the stalwart manor caught in a whirlwind of change, replete with cat puns and regal costumes. As its book blurb says, "the fur will fly."

We highly recommend this literary cat treat. It's an absolute hoot and beautifully executed. We recommend ordering a copy forthwith from your nearest *purr-veyor* of fine reading materials.

8 - Cats Who Meant Business

Britain's Commercial Success

The rise of the British Empire was predicated on the unparalleled reach of trade and colonialism achieved by the English between the 17th and 19th centuries. And, as we shall soon learn, cats played their part in this commercial enterprise.

The Navy's Seafaring Felines

The Royal Navy is the oldest of the British armed forces and, as a result, is called the Senior Service. At one point, this very British institution maintained the most extensive fleet of naval ships in the world. Ship's cats' are not unique to the Royal Navy because pest control, especially of mice and rats, was crucial to successful voyages the world over. However, the ship cats of the British Navy are legendary for many reasons. They were banned from official ships in 1975 (some sourpuss cited "hygiene" as the reason), perhaps forgetting that carefully washing and grooming themselves is any self-respecting cat's favorite pastime. However, before that time, some naval cats achieved a measurable level of fame in a number of fascinating ways.

Perhaps Britain's greatest naval hero was Admiral Nelson. He joined the Royal Navy as a mere boy of 12. Nelson's final great victory was at the Battle of Trafalgar, where he was fatally wounded by a French bullet. Therefore, it was with great interest that we came to hear accounts of Nelson's cat Tiddles. This kitty was initially featured in a 1990 issue of The Spectator magazine. In it, Guy Evans, a National Trust employee, wrote about the cat's early life as an abandoned kitten who was found at the British Embassy in Naples and taken in by Nelson's mistress Emma Hamilton, who lived at the Embassy.

According to Evans, Tiddles gradually came to be admired

both by those at the Embassy and by the royals at the court of Naples, helping to guarantee friendly relations between Naples and Britain. The kitty was then supposedly taken back to Britain by Nelson and his mistress, who presumably must have cared about him a great deal to have taken him all that way.

Evans's story in The Spectator magazine went on to recount that Tiddles was present at the Battle of Trafalgar, where the kitty was noted for his insouciant, fearless air as the fighting raged all around him. This story was picked up and repeated by numerous sources in the press, featured as a topic on a TV quiz show, and included by tour guides relating incidents from Nelson's life aboard his ship (now a museum), the *HMS Victory*.

However, in 2005, Evans's widow revealed that the whole story (accompanied by very real-seeming footnotes) had been an elaborate hoax. We're not sure which we were most amused by, that Evans had crafted such an adorably cat-centric story or that the British public, including some distinguished scholars, had been taken in by the tall tale.

However, not all British naval cats were fictional inventions.

A famous photograph shows Winston Churchill patting a tuxedo cat named Blackie, who was the ship's cat on the HMS *Prince of Wales*. Churchill patted Blackie to stop him from making his way from the British boat to a neighboring American vessel. In the statesman's honor, the wandering kitty was renamed "Churchill" soon afterward.

There were other famed naval cats, such as Convoy, who was adorably photographed as a morale booster in World War II. A newspaper photograph showed this cute kitty being gazed at adoringly by the crew of HMS Hermione as he dozed in a miniature hammock carefully crafted for him. Sadly, both the sailors and their cat were torpedoed by a German submarine in 1942. We salute the brave heroes who gave their lives to secure peace on the high seas.

Lest you think the British navy only welcome moggies onboard during wartime, there were some noted felines in peacetime. For instance, there were ambassador cats, such as Felix, who sailed aboard the Mayflower II to promote post-war British and American relations. Then there was Wunpound Cat, who accompanied the crew of the HMS *Hecate* for eight years before being forced into retirement by the 1975 ban on cats aboard naval vessels. The cat was so named because he was a little stray, found at the shelter and bought for a mere one pound ($1.20 at the time of writing). Ah, Wunpound, the last of the Royal Navy's noble feline tradition! Maybe, someday the Royal Navy will see the error of their ways and welcome cats onboard once again...

Not all feline associations with the British navy were pleasant. You may have heard the expression, "there's not enough room in here to swing a cat!" This expression came from the cat-o'-nine-tails, a whip-like instrument of punishment that was used to brutalize unruly sailors on naval ships.

However, this whip was too long to use below deck (not enough room to swing a "cat"), so it had to be used on deck to flog the bare backs of unfortunate sailors. A cat-o'-nine-tails gets its name, by the way, from the scars it left, which looked like they'd been left by a cat's scratches.

We'd just like to make it clear though that no actual cats were used in inflicting this punishment. Maybe we're being too naïve and sentimental here, but we'd like to think that a cuddle from a ship's cat might have been some comfort to those who suffered such brutal torture.

Dick Whittington's Cat

From its start as the central trading post of Londinium during Roman times, through its development as an imperial world power, London has drawn people from all over the globe, looking for economic opportunities and personal enrichment. The legend of Dick Whittington and his cat embodies such a rags-to-riches story—and it stars a pretty pussycat! Or does it? Read on to find out more...

Essentially, the story goes something like this: Dick Whittington was an orphan who hoped to make his fortune in London. Before he arrived there, he believed that the streets were paved with gold, so outrageous were the tales about London's bountiful wealth. However, when Whittington arrived there, he was taken aback by the exploitation he endured at the hands of his employer and the fact that many people lived in abject poverty.

The story tells us that Whittington was asked by his master to allow his cat to sail on one of his trading ships to help control the rat population on board. Dick was unhappy about this, but he relented and let his cat go. Whittington's misery was so intense that, without the cat's company, his mistreatment ate away at him until he decided to run away and leave London for good.

However, as Whittington reached Highgate Hill—the point at which nowadays is located a statue of his cat—he heard the bells pealing and thought they said, "Turn again, Whittington, Lord Mayor of London." So, he returned to the city, only to find out that his amazing cat had done his job so well that he fetched a fortune from a Moorish ruler on the Barbary coast whose court was overrun with rats. Thus, Dick Whittington was now rather a wealthy chap who went on to marry the merchant's daughter, increased his fortune through canny deals, and eventually became Lord Mayor of London. Interestingly, the real adventures of Dick Whittington are different from this commonly-told tale.

It seems Whittington was not an impoverished jack-the-lad but the son of a knight from Gloucestershire who went to London to become an influential merchant. The "cat" in the legend refers to the dubious way Whittington conducted business. This wily merchant's success relied heavily on the distribution of bribes—which in the Middle English of the day were called "achat" (pronounced "a cat" by the English and coming from the French word for "purchases").

Thus, the legend of Wellington's remarkable rise to wealth and power was born -all due to "a cat." A portrait of Whittington was altered to show him resting his hand on a cat, something that might have been an insider pun at the time but was later mistakenly interpreted to refer to an actual feline.

Britain's Shop Cats

Cats have been a constant presence in British shops providing rodent patrol and companionship to both shopkeepers and customers. Britain has long been described as "a nation of shopkeepers." Coined perhaps by the Scottish economist Adam Smith, the phrase was intended to convey how the British were skilled at and eager to benefit from the rewards of trade.

This phrase is often nowadays (and perhaps inaccurately) attributed to Napoleon as an insulting sneer at the British for their attention to essential commercial matters rather than to the more grandiose projects that Bonaparte himself undertook. Still, it has to be said that many great British shops, such as Fortnum & Mason, with its legendary hampers stocked to the brim with British culinary treats and dispatched to all corners of the world, have long outlasted the pint-sized French military legend. Take that, Napoleon! Nowadays, many British entrepreneurs create and sell products related to cats. I'm particularly partial to katzenworld.shop, which offers an astounding array of cat-related goods that ship not only in Britain but also internationally.

The late British Prime Minister Margaret Thatcher herself was proud to be a grocer's daughter from the small town of Grantham, where shop cats would have been a common phenomenon. In fact, during her term as Prime Minister, she once reportedly purchased a can of sardines in Moscow as a present to bring home to the official cat of 10 Downing Street, the Prime Minister's residence. Talk about using capitalism to upstage the communists! It also shows in what high esteem she must have held the cat that matters of international importance didn't prevent her from thinking about what the kitty might have for his supper!

Beatrix's book *The Tale of Ginger and Pickles* supports the notion that both shopkeepers and cats play an essential role in British life. In this anthropomorphized morality tale from 1909, Potter writes about the village shop run by Ginger the cat and Pickles the Terrier. She relates the struggles of these generous business owners who extend so much credit to their customers that they are forced to close down. The shop's demise is hastened by the fact that Ginger the feline shopkeeper drools every time a mouse customer visits, while Pickles the dog can't help but bark at the rabbit customers.

Eventually, the shop is reopened under the stewardship of the more sensible Sally Henny-Penny (a chicken). While we appreciate the intention to impart good sense to young children, we bristle at the implication that a cat can't handle a shop's business. Indeed, it's downright daft to suggest that cats (or dogs) would possess less commercial ability than poultry. This is one of the few points on which cats and dogs are in agreement!

Crest of the Scottish Clan Chattan, which has the cat as their emblem

The Romans and *Felis Catus*

Roman legions brought the domestic cat with them into Northern Europe as they expanded their empire northwards. The famous general Julius Caesar thought it was a wise move to teach the barbarous Britons a lesson for siding with some anti-Roman Gauls in what is now France. So, he invaded Britain in 43AD.

One can only imagine the scene: Roman carriages laden with supplies of dormice, a delicacy of Roman cuisine, along with their beloved fermented fish sauce, garum. Me-ow! How could the cats resist tagging along? However, once they arrived in Britain, these cats—who were used to basking on sun-warmed Roman flagstones—must have looked around disappointedly at the rain-sodden landscape, pondering whether they'd done the right thing. But by quickly taking on a typically British attitude, we're sure they adopted a stiff upper lip and decided to "bloody well get on with it."

When the Roman Empire finally collapsed, some 1600 years ago, the cats the Romans had introduced to Britain remained.

By this stage, we must presume that the cats had made themselves thoroughly at home on that cold and damp isle of some three and a half million potential cat lovers. Surely, they must have missed the Roman innovation of central heating—air vented under the floor of their villas. The Romans had built cities, like Londinium, which comprised mazes of streets and alleys for the cat's favorite prey, rats and mice. Furthermore, the Romans had brought an agricultural industry that kept cats working hard on farms, protecting grain stores from vermin. The Roman Empire might have retreated, but its cats and their descendants remained.

Life Among the Anglo-Saxons

The Anglo Saxons came from Northern Europe and settled in England during the fifth and sixth centuries. They were from three major Germanic tribes with rather musical names, the Angles, Saxons, and Jutes. These newcomers spread across the low-lying fertile lands in South-Eastern Britain, taking advantage of the power vacuum that came about once the Romans left Britain in the early fifth century.

In Anglo-Saxon households, it seems clear that cats were kept as pets. In an archaeological dig in East Sussex, the remains of a well-fed cat with a belly full of fish were discovered alongside other less-favored kitties who were likely working mousers rather than pampered pets.

There is evidence in the Anglo-Saxon divorce laws that humans were attached to their kitties. Legal texts from this time give clear guidance on allocating one cat to the newly divorced woman and one to her husband.

Regarding other animals in Anglo-Saxon times, mice were the same size, but rats were smaller black rats, not the larger brown rat of modern times. We're not sure whether Anglo-Saxon kitties were happy to have less intimidating rats to tackle or disappointed that they didn't get as much to munch on. Even the more substantial Anglo-Saxon dwellings were rather unimposing wooden structures. Lighting was generally provided by little pots of grease in which a few threads of linen were placed as a wick. We wonder if any Anglo-Saxon kitties got into trouble for nibbling on the grease pots and causing the household to curse them when they were deprived of much-needed lighting after dark?

The Norman Conquest

In 1066, Anglo-Saxon rule was disrupted by the invasion of William, the Duke of Normandy, along with his French armies, in what came to be known as the Norman Conquest.

One of the most significant impacts that the Normans had on English culture was the rise of the Norman castle. These castles were essentially self-supporting strongholds of the power that housed dozens, if not hundreds of people.

Naturally, castles were home to many animals kept for agricultural needs and domestic duties. These fortified precincts were self-contained so that humans and animals alike could shelter for more extended periods if under attack. Aside from farm animals like cows and pigs, or working animals like horses and mules, domesticated dogs and cats were kept as pets or wandered about as strays.

The new stone Norman moat and bailey castles, of which approximately 700 were built across the land, allowed the installation of sturdy stone fireplaces that radiated far more heat than Anglo-Saxon fire pits in the center of the dwelling. We're sure this innovation was appreciated by humans and felines alike. Life was quite a bit more comfortable for those (human and feline) fortunate enough to be among the new Norman ruling classes.

Most of the Norman castle dungeons were used not so much for imprisoning people as for hoarding vast quantities of food in preparation for a siege. We're sure the cats within the castle walls took gladly to protecting these foodstuffs from rodents as well as maybe (and we did say maybe!) pilfering an odd morsel or two.

As time went on and the Normans returned from the early crusades to the Middle East, they brought luxurious fabrics, such as silks and other cloths, which were made into comfy cushions and sumptuous wall hangings. This sophisticated domestic setup was all rather alluring for the kitties who managed to insinuate themselves into the Normans' good graces.

The Norman influence in Britain has been a lasting one and has set the tone for how the upper-class English conduct themselves to the present day. The sprucely, clean-shaven Normans only enjoyed fur on kittens and other pets, not on their faces. Their dining rituals emphasized a new and fussier etiquette—one could compare it to the difference between a dog at his chow and a cat lapping up her Fancy Feast. The Normans also introduced more pork, and perhaps more to their cats' taste, rabbits to the menu.

Howell The Good's Humane Laws

Hywel Dda, anglicized as Howell the Good, was the most prominent king of medieval Wales, recognized both for his regulation of Welsh law and for his strategically self-interested capitulation to the English. His laws were considered very fair, and thus, he was known as " Howell the Good." Cats, of course, know that he was a decent sort because he clearly recognized their unparalleled worth, enacting *actual laws* regarding a feline's value.

According to Howell the Good's laws, a kitten's value from the time of its birth to when it had opened its eyes was a penny, an amount that would buy two dozen two-pound loaves of good bread. By the time a kitten had grown sufficiently to feed on mice (and keep those blasted rodents under control), its worth doubled to two pennies. A cat that fed on mice was worth four pennies under Howell's rule, nearly as much as an entire pig. We're sure that any mother cat of the age worth her salt would have passed on the knowledge of Howell's compassionate laws to her kittens. One imagines that these grateful cats laid mice at the castle gates in tribute to the goodness of Howell.

9 - A LONG AND DISTINGUISHED HISTORY

Henry VIII's Pet-Crazy Court

Many young girls have fantasized about marrying a prince. While such daydreams might be a pleasant way of passing the time—be wary! Sometimes such dreams can turn into nightmares. Witness Henry VIII, who had six wives, whose fates are recounted in the following rhyme: "Divorced, Beheaded, Died / Divorced, Beheaded, Survived." Mmmm, not a very good track record. Perhaps he would have done better to take on some cats. At least cats have nine lives!

Henry VIII ruled England for more than 35 years in the sixteenth century. His decision to annul his first marriage to facilitate his second marriage led to the Church of England setting itself up independently of the Catholic Church, which was ruled by Rome.

Pet keeping was a widespread practice at Henry's court, and such companion animals were treated lavishly. Catherine of Aragon, Henry's first wife, apparently had a pet monkey. It was also quite fashionable to keep songbirds, especially for the ladies at court. There must have been a profusion of melody—not to mention a fair number of cats whose ears often perked up in interest at the prospect of a tasty little songbird as a snack.

Yet cats were still under suspicion for their purported association with witches and evil intentions, as superstitions still abounded, thus making dogs the favored pet of the age. Henry VIII was enormously fond of dogs, dressed them in decorative collars, and adorned them with pearls and other finery—try doing *that* with your cat. Wear sturdy gloves if you're bold enough to try!

Of course, my interest is primarily in cats, and I wanted to know if, despite their poor reputation at the time, any cats had made their way into Henry's court. So, while doing research for this book, I was intrigued to come across a mention of Henry owning a cat called Dagobert, for whom he had designed a special suit of armor so that this plucky feline could accompany him on his military adventures.

However, no matter how much I wished it to be accurate, this tale turns out to be the fanciful invention of Canadian artist Jeff de Boer, who sculpts suits of armor for cats (and mice). He created a fictional backstory for Dagobert, claiming that he was the military companion of Henry VIII. Perhaps you could contact Jeff to commission a protective outfit if your little mite is prone to scuffles with other neighborhood kitties...

Although Henry and his wives may not have kept cats, at least one highly influential figure at the court is reported to have done so. Cardinal Wolsey, one of the principal (if ultimately doomed) advisors to Henry VIII, was said to have dearly loved his feline companions. Legend has it that he thought so highly of them that he took them with him to almost every formal occasion he attended. Given that he was the King's Chief Minister, the occasions must have been numerous and the pomp overwhelming. Whether his cats would have been delighted by all the ceremony and glamour or grudgingly put up with being paraded around is anyone's guess.

Cardinal Wolsey's cats even accompanied him to church services. While there is no physical piece of evidence (like a painting) to show the close bond he shared with his cats, there are undoubtedly many accounts that attest to such. However, there is also the possibility that reports of him being accompanied by cats were a slur upon his reputation during a time when cats were often associated with witchcraft and evil-doing.

Wolsey was ultimately accused of treason and sentenced to death. He was spared execution by an untimely death of supposed "natural causes." What happened to his cats following his death is unknown. We can only hope that those loyal felines scampered away after his passing, fleeing these corrupted corridors of power for a peaceful refuge in the country, far from court intrigue.

Elizabeth I's Not-So Glorious Reign

Elizabeth I (1533-1603) was Henry VIII's daughter by his second wife, Anne Boleyn, who was branded an adulteress and beheaded on Henry's orders when Elizabeth was only two years old. What a start in life for the young princess Elizabeth, eh? Presumably recovered from such childhood trauma, Elizabeth eventually ascended to the throne and consolidated England's move toward becoming a Protestant nation. Although lauded as a golden age for England, it was generally a dark period for its cats.

The queen's coronation procession featured an enormous wicker representation of the Pope filled with live cats. This was paraded through the city of London before being set on fire! This barbaric display indicated that the superstitious association of cats with evil was still going strong. By extension, the association of Catholicism with fiendish practices was also reinforced. The Protestant Reformation sought to establish a new church free of the corruption hitherto attributed to Catholicism, and cats were just unfortunate, uh, "scape cats."

Lest we unfairly taint Protestantism as the exclusive repository of cat hatred and persecution, it's wise to bear in mind that cruelty towards cats was common at the time, having been spurred to some extent by an edict by Pope Gregory IX way back in the 1200s.

Furthermore, hateful treatment of animals was not restricted to cats. Those who nowadays long wistfully for the good old days often underestimate how arbitrarily cruel and bloody such long-gone times were—both for all kinds of animals and indeed for humans. Let's not forget the brutal manner in which Elizabeth dealt with those suspected of acting against her. Burning heretics—those who refused to acknowledge the new Church of England—was a common practice of hers.

The many potential threats to her power required Elizabeth

to be mindful of her rivals and enemies. Her cousin Mary, Queen of Scots posed a potential danger as a rival claimant to the throne. Mary was kept under strict control by Elizabeth in luxurious house arrest. Mary found the imprisonment torturous and tried to while away the long, dreary days with ladylike pursuits such as needlework. One of the Queen of Scots' surviving embroidery panels depicts a ginger cat tormenting a mouse, an allusion perhaps to how Mary felt about being kept captive by Elizabeth I, perhaps the most famous ginger-tressed lady of her time.

Ruthless and harsh as many of her actions may have been, Elizabeth was a strong ruler who established a period of stability. During her reign, the economy prospered, many scientific discoveries were made, and the wealthy built grand mansions, which boasted the hitherto unimaginable luxury of many large glass windows. Glass blowing was a laborious, tricky, and thus expensive process. Hardwick Hall, built by Bess of Hardwick, one of the wealthiest women in England, was said to be "more glass than wall." We wonder how many kitties enjoyed these new fancy windows, both for a chance to gaze at what was going on outside and as another means by which to wander in and out of these grand houses – as cats are so fond of doing...

The Stuarts' Rather Unlucky Cat

After the long and prosperous Elizabethan period, James I, who was also the king of Scotland, took the throne, joining together the previously warring nations and establishing the Stuart dynasty. Although there were some threats to his power, James maintained peace. However, this was followed by a more turbulent period, with the crowning of King Charles I and his autocratic rule.

Charles's high-handedness ultimately led to a bloody civil war. The parliamentary forces under Cromwell won and imprisoned the monarch for treason. Legend has it, however, that Charles had a black cat by his side who he was convinced would make everything alright. Well, cats generally do, don't they?

The cat was named "Lucky," and Charles doted on it, convinced the kitty was guaranteeing him good fortune. However, the cat went missing on the day before Charles was finally executed. Let this be a lesson to cat-loving tyrants everywhere, don't let your kitty out of your sight! The monarchy was dissolved—and the very Puritan Oliver Cromwell rose to power, becoming Lord Protectorate over the newly formed Commonwealth of England.

Cromwell initiated the closing of all theaters in England and banned singing from churches. To say he was a sourpuss is quite the understatement! Eventually, Parliament decided to restore the monarchy. With the Restoration, Charles II presided over one of the most hedonistic periods in British history, with much extravagant behavior unleashed as a reaction to the long, somber period of Puritan rule. Gentlemen took to adorning themselves in lace collars and luxurious fabrics. These foppish dandies groomed themselves more excessively than even the most prideful of Persian pussycats.

While Charles II was very fond of dogs—the Cavalier King Charles Spaniel is a breed named for the restored king—cats did not get much respect during this period. In fact, when the Black Plague again came knocking on England's door, most of the cats were deliberately destroyed. It was believed that cats spread the plague, so they were systematically killed throughout London and elsewhere.

The result of this was a *cat-astrophe* as the rats who carried the fleas that carried the plague thrived, and, thus, the epidemic became worse. It wasn't until the Great Fire of London in September 1666 that most of the plague was completely burned out of the city.

Georgian Cat Lovers

The Georgian period heralded the arrival of humanitarianism, with its greater consideration towards one's fellow creatures—human and non-human. Cats did feature prominently in the popular imagination, as evidenced by an anonymous story published in 1760 called "The Life and Adventures of a Cat." The hero of this story was a male cat named Tom. The tale became very popular and led to the widespread usage of tomcat to describe a male kitty. The latter part of the Georgian era is known as The Regency when George III's son ruled as regent on his ill father's behalf.

This Regency period is renowned for its simple and elegant fashion and style, captured evocatively in the novels of Jane Austen, in which her non-human focus is mainly on the noble horsepower pulling various status-enhancing carriages, with some mention of dogs occasionally. From my research, I believe that Austen's only mention of cats is in a private letter where she described a fleeting glimpse of a solitary black kitten slipping away down a staircase inside her lodgings in Bath. For me, this seemingly insignificant anecdote bears witness to the fact that, even when not expressly mentioned, cats are always there, slinking about the outer limits of our consciousness.

Throughout the Georgian period, attitudes toward domesticated animals were changing. Superstitious views of cats began to be tempered by more enlightened ideas about pets and more humane treatment of animals. Pets came to occupy a more central role in the culture. The poet Thomas Grey penned an elegy to one of his pet cats in 1748, while painters such as Joseph Wright and Charlotte Jones captured kittens at play and elegant cats in fancy drawing rooms. Wright's paintings show that our love for dressing up cats extends far back into history, with his images of young girls playing with a pussycat as if it were a doll! So all you cat dresser-uppers out there, this pursuit is nothing new...

Queen Vicktoria's Kitties

Queen Victoria was the Queen of the United Kingdom between 1837 and 1901. She and her husband Albert had nine children. Their home life, including the royal family's fondness for pets, was widely emulated. There was a considerable rise in living conditions and home comforts during the Victorian period. The era's décor was cozy and cluttered with many velvet cushions on which cats could daintily perch, feasting their eyes on decorative china ornaments that are so irresistible to paw at.

The Queen was an avid cat lover. It's said her lifelong love of cats originated with a gift of a kitten from an impoverished old lady who implored the queen to care for the cat. Queen Victoria did so, and she sent the woman a thank you note and ten pounds (worth around $1,500 in today's money!).

During her life, Queen Victoria offered a warm and loving home to many felines, such as Peter, a black cat who is said to have inspired Edgar Allen Poe to pen the story "The Black Cat." Victoria requested that the Royal Society for the Protection of Cruelty to Animals add a cat to its Medal of Kindness. Her patronage launched the society on its way to provide advocacy and support for animal causes right up to the present day.

Prince Albert, Victoria's beloved husband, was also a lover of animals. The two presided over the founding of the country's first zoos. Queen Victoria was delighted by exotic animals, including the powerful feline grace of the big cats, such as leopards. In a letter, she wrote delightedly about a lion cub that a domestic cat was raising. She wrote excitedly about the spectacle of seeing the cub "suck out of a bottle, like a baby!"

Toward the end of her life, the queen had a cat named White Heather, whom she clearly loved. The white and fluffy cat was probably either a Persian or an Angora. Victoria left instructions for the cat to continue living a life of royal splendor at Buckingham Palace even after she herself had died. Nonetheless, White Heather's splendid status was probably somewhat more regal than the other feline occupants of the palace. The "downstairs kitties" presumably skulked about the chilly servants' quarters while uniformed lackeys rang a bell for treats to be brought to White Heather from the kitchen.

9 - A LONG AND DISTINGUISHED HISTORY

Voting Rights for Cat Ladies

Between 1900 and 1918, women in Britain struggled to earn voting rights. Opponents of this 'suffragette' movement published the "Orthochrome," a series of postcards intended to mock women's desire for equal treatment. For instance, one postcard called "The Advocate for Women's Rights" featured a plump, grey cat wearing a feathered sun hat and striped shawl in the suffragists' symbolic colors of purple, white, and green.

Such postcards featuring cute kitties were sent to prominent campaigners in the movement to mock them and emphasize how cute, and by extension, trivial their concerns were. Women voters eventually triumphed, and the kitty postcards' attempts to ridicule the suffragettes failed. Women finally attained their civil voting rights in 1918. We assume that when victory was announced cat ladies throughout Britain celebrated with a toast of milk in the company of their furry companions...

Cats in The Colonies

It is widely stated that the British Empire once was so large that the sun never set upon it. That is, at some point in any 24 hours, the sun was shining on a plot of land held by the British Crown, which in 1913 covered approximately 25% of the countries in the world. While lions stalked the vast savannas of Africa and tigers hunted in the dense forests of Asia, British expatriates and imperial rulers overseas were often more focused on the smaller, more domestic felines than you might have imagined.

It's interesting to note that the British bred cats in the Empire to prevent plague outbreaks. They called the scheme "animal technology," and it was promoted in the early 20th century as a means to improve public health in India and beyond. A cat farm was even established in what the British termed "Burma," now known as Myanmar. Local newspapers, however, lamented that the farm spent more money on food and upkeep for cats than was spent on curing local lepers.

However, it's ironic that while small, cuddly domestic cats were being idolized on home soil, their larger cousins were being hunted for their pelts throughout the British Empire. Big game hunting was admired for the skill and so-called "manliness" involved, and the trophies gained (in the form of skins, skulls, tusks, etc.) graced many an aristocratic manor hall back in Britain.

A large part of the British imperialist mission (apart from conquering new territories and "bringing them into the fold") was to map hitherto uncharted territories. This involved voyages of discovery, some of which had an essential feline connection.

One intrepid kitty who was part of British imperial expansion was a kitty by the name of Trim. This cat was born in 1799 aboard a ship making the voyage from the Cape of Good Hope in South Africa to Botany Bay in what is now the harbor in Sydney, Australia. Right from the start, the kitten was noted for his pluck. For instance, Trim fell overboard in rough seas but was able to paddle his way furiously back to the vessel and climb up a rope to get back on the ship. From that day on, he was the favorite of the captain, one Mr. Flinders, and of the rest of the crew. Trim became inseparable from his new master, and Flinders took him with him on a voyage on *HMS Investigator*. This ship's mission was to sail around Australia, charting a map of its coastline. Flinders and Trim survived shipwreck in1803, and when Flinders was suspected of spying by the French in Mauritius, Trim loyally shared his human friend's captivity until Flinders' eventual release.

Part of Flinders' epitaph to Trim describes him thus: "the most...faithful of servants and best of creatures. He made the tour of the globe, and a voyage to Australia." Trim has been immortalized in public sculptures in London, Lincolnshire, and in two locations in Australia.

Not all British kitties explored warm oceans; some took part in chillier adventures. One such frigid foray was Ernest Shackleton's grandly-named Imperial Trans-Antarctic expedition of 1914-1917. Its goal was to be the first to make a land crossing of the icy Antarctic continent. Although this goal was not reached, Shackleton and his crew were pioneers in exploring the bleak, frozen landscapes. As is often the case with such derring-do expeditions, there were harsh setbacks, not to mention tragedies.

One especially sad episode involves a ship's cat intriguingly named Mrs. Chippy. Now, at the time, the term 'chippy' was a widely used nickname for a carpenter. The ship's carpenter aboard the expedition's ship was a fellow by the name of McNish. The ship's tiger-striped tabby followed the carpenter around like a devoted wife. This relationship was noticed, and even though the cat was male, the crew took to calling the kitty "Mrs. Chippy."

Apart from shadowing his carpenter friend everywhere he went on board, Mrs. Chippy was a natural seafarer, walking inch-wide rails nimbly without falling, even in the roughest of seas. Furthermore, the cat would scale the ship's rigging just as quickly and skillfully as a trained human sailor. The cat's escapades were documented in the diaries of several crew members, including the episode when he jumped overboard by mistake and the ship turned around to pick him up. Even though he had been ten minutes in the raging seas, the brave pussycat emerged unharmed.

However, the brave Mrs. Chippy met a sorrowful end when the ship, *The Endurance,* was trapped in pack ice, and the expedition seemed doomed. Shackleton decided the most merciful action would be to shoot five of the sled dogs and Mrs. Chippy. This brutal act seemed the lesser of two evils as the limited provisions meant the animals were probably going to starve to death. Shackleton, the expedition leader, recorded in his diary that the crew, especially the cat-loving carpenter, were distraught. The craftsman never forgave Shackleton for killing his feline friend. In 1930, the poor McNish died penniless in Wellington, New Zealand. Although he was buried with full naval honors, McNish's grave was originally unmarked. However, this oversight was corrected in 1959 when a headstone was erected. In 2004, a life-sized statue of Mrs. Chippy was placed on the grave, reuniting the carpenter and the cat in a touchingly bittersweet way. This fondly-remembered feline and his courageous life have also been commemorated by novels, films, stamps, paintings, and even an opera for schoolchildren.

Rudyard Kipling and Controversy

One of the most famous English writers of the 19th and early 20th centuries, Kipling was the first British author to win the Nobel Prize for literature. His views regarding the empire and colonialism might seem downright illogical or hateful to us; he famously penned "The White Man's Burden." This poem expressed the view that the "white man" should paternalistically care for the "darker" races.

Yet, some stories and books of Kipling's display a more balanced understanding of the nature of colonialism. For example, *The Man Who Would Be King* details the folly of foiled imperial attempts. The writer was also known for his largely kindly fascination with animals, from the exotic to the domestic, including all kinds of felines.

Just about everyone is familiar with Kipling's *The Jungle Book*, whether it be from the original book or the beloved Disney film version with its cast of anthropomorphized animal characters. The ruthless big cat Shere Khan (loosely, "King Tiger") stalks the pages with his menacing yet regal presence.

Kipling had great respect for the feline traits of independence and self-possession. There is clear evidence of this in his short story "The Cat That Walked By Himself." The story revolves around the cat's assertion of his superiority over other domesticated animals, a lofty position earned by the cat due to his independence and intelligence. The cat will not be easily tamed like other animals – he wanders at will and does not follow commands. Yet he also enjoys the company of people. The cat has it all, being praised for purring the baby to sleep and for catching a mouse. In return the kitty can enjoy the comfort of the fire and a warm bowl of milk. However, the feline comes and goes as he pleases, unlike the poor dog who has made a deal with humankind that places the canine in a beloved yet subservient position. Kipling clearly admires such feline savvy, as do most of us, I'm sure...

British Eccentricity

The British like to go their own way, much like our feline friends. Whole books have been written on the subject of British eccentrics. Anyone who has witnessed the pioneering humor of Monty Python, the decades-long dominance of the weirdly popular *Doctor Who* franchise, or the grandstanding antics of British politicians on the Parliament floor knows that the Brits—like the cat company they keep—don't always care much what others think of them. Here are some endearing English eccentrics who happen to love cats as much as we do.

Lear's Homesick Cat

Writer and illustrator Edward Lear famously penned "The Owl and the Pussy-Cat" nonsense poem, where the oddly-matched pair "dance by the light of the moon" after the Owl profusely declares his love for the Pussy-Cat. Many of Lear's stories and drawings were inspired by his real-life tabby cat, Foss.

When Lear moved from England to Italy in later life, he instructed his architect to reproduce his English home as closely as possible—so that the poor kitty would not be too fussed about the relocation and wouldn't miss dear old England too much. Of course, when old Foss died—at the respectable age of 17, plump and pampered—he was given a full funeral and buried in Lear's Italian garden. Notably, the author died only a few months after the demise of his cherished cat.

The Naming Game

A prolific 20th-century British composer, playwright, and author, Beverley Nichols penned works on a wide variety of subjects and wrote more than 50 books. He was an enthusiastic fan of felines, including them in many of his works and even writing some pieces specifically about cats. Oddly enough, he disliked the term "cat lover." He believed that the term indicated he didn't have any love for other animals —untrue, he claimed, even though cats were his special favorites.

Nichols coined the monikers "F" and "non-F" to indicate whether people were "feline or non-feline by nature." This naming convention is reminiscent of his contemporary Nancy Mitford's designations of "U" and "non-U" to distinguish who was upper class from who was definitely not.

Nichols assigned his cats numbers instead of names. He claimed this habit was inspired by the global success of Chanel's No. 5 perfume. He said that because of this achievement, "numbers have acquired a subtle elegance of their own"—presumably like his lithe felines.

Nichols started his pride with a Siamese who was named

Number One. He then acquired Numbers Two through Five. He skipped Six (it sounded too much like the cat was ill: "Sicks"). He resumed with Number Seven. Number Eight was originally named Oscar before Nichols adopted him, so the confused cat was called by both names. Not content to stop there, Nichols wrote that he would yet find "Nine, Ten, Eleven and Twelve, who are sleeping somewhere in the womb of time." A true cat lover, he admitted, "I have a catholic taste in cats, in the sense that anything feline on four legs goes straight to my heart."I'm sure that so many of us would agree!

The House of Shame

The Cat House is a tourist attraction in the picturesque English county of Sussex. Its 18th-century owner, an eccentric gentleman by the name of Bob Ward, kept a pet canary. One sad day, the canary escaped from its cage, flying out of the window just as local priest Nathanial Woodward was passing by with his cat. Alas, as you can imagine, the cat made short work of the canary! Ward was furious and wanted to remind the clergyman forever of what his cat had done. So, he decided that he would alter his dwelling to bear witness to the murder of his beloved songbird by the dastardly kitty.

The house in question had a thatched roof, and its walls were a traditional English mix of white plaster and dark timber. The homeowner (at not inconsiderable expense) created metal cats (complete with canaries in their wicked paws), which he placed around the building, strung together with bells that would jangle anytime the cat-owning clergyman would pass by. The cats are still there, and the bells no longer chastise passing clergymen but now merrily welcome visitors to the charming house whose façade is enhanced by some typically English climbing roses. The cat-themed dwelling is well worth visiting if you're ever in Sussex.

Leaving It All to The Cats' Home

"I'm leaving it all to the cats' home!" has been a common refrain among curmudgeonly Brits who feel underappreciated by their nearest and dearest humans. Indeed, many British eccentrics—including some quite famous ones—have done just that, leaving vast sums of money to what are undoubtedly the most pampered pets of all time.

Freddie Mercury, the eccentric rock genius who founded the band *Queen* fame, absolutely adored cats, as well as his former girlfriend, Mary Austin. He dedicated one of his solo albums, "Mr. Bad Guy," to his cats "and all the cat lovers across the universe." When he died in 1991, he left the bulk of his enormous estate to Miss Austin along with instructions on how to care for his cats after his passing.

Some lesser-known British eccentrics have also named their cats in their wills. Ben Rea, an antiques dealer who died in 1988, decided not to leave even a penny to his human relatives. Instead, he left the bulk of his $12.5 million fortune to his cat, Blackie, and to three different cat charities.

In 2023 Londoner Margaret Layne left nearly a million dollars to a former stray cat, Tinker. She also specified which treats the cat should receive and stated that her house not be sold until the event of Tinker's death so as not to disturb the cat's comfort. A trust fund was left to Mrs. Layne's neighbors, Mr. and Mrs. Wheatly, so that they could maintain the house and look after the cat. It seems that the Wheatley's own cat Lucy left their home to move in with the now-wealthy Tinker. The pair of cats frequently feed on the traditional British fishy treat of coley (or coalfish), of which they are offered only the very freshest examples. Let me tell you, if I get to be reincarnated, I wouldn't mind coming back as the beloved cat of a wealthy British eccentric!

" ARRIVED SAFELY."

Cats And the Railways

The first-ever passenger-carrying public railway in Britain opened in 1807. It was delightfully named the Swansea and Mumbles Railway and the carriages were horse-drawn. It's hard to imagine nowadays how revolutionary the advent of more extensive railway networks was. Travel times by rail were sometimes twice as fast and half as expensive as by road.

12 - TRAVEL AND TOURISM

The British railways were the Internet of their day, making goods quickly and widely available and bringing people together in ways previously undreamed of. The railways popularised leisure pursuits such as hiking in the country and trips to the seaside. Additionally, the railways opened up access for village and townsfolk to the big city, with its more abundant employment and commercial opportunities.

Down through the years, the railways of Britain have had many fascinating connections with cats. For example, a stray cat named Tiddles "worked" in the 1970s and 80s in the London Railway station's ladies' room at Paddington station. Popularly known as the "peeping Tom," the tabby used to squeeze under the stall doors trying to make the acquaintance of the poor startled ladies! Tsk, tsk! He weighed about 25 pounds owing to the ample diet of lamb, cod, and steak provided by his admirers. The rude intruder became so well known that he used to receive fan mail from across the globe.

When it comes to cats and railway stations in Britain, Stan is another name to note. Diz White, the author of the charming 2016 tale of English Life, *More Cotswold Memoirs,* describes the antics of this tabby cat who lived at

Oxfordshire's Charlbury train station. The friendly kitty was often spotted sitting in the lap of the travelers while they waited for their train to arrive. If not sitting on somebody's lap, Stan the cat could be seen sleeping on the ground under the ticket booth window. This likable pussycat made his presence known and became an integral part of the train station. Stan was such a popular lap cat that a painting of him was hung on the main wall of the railway office. The loveable tabby would also watch fish swimming in the lily pond close to the railway platform. It seems this kitty liked to mix up his routine and avail of all the attractions on offer!

Another notable railway feline goes by the name of Hi-Vis. This ginger kitty made herself at home in the Inverness train station in the Scottish Highlands from March 2012 onwards. Named for the fluorescent "high visibility" jackets worn by workers on the railway line, Hi-Vis won the hearts of the railway station staff. The adorable feline loved rubbing against the legs of the passengers and lying in their laps until their train arrived. To say she was pretty popular among the workers and visitors alike would be an understatement.

However, Hi-Vis was not the only kitty to grace the platforms at Inverness. This Sottish train station is also famous for other cats with railway-related names like Diesel and Gasket, to name a few.

However, perhaps the most famous British railway cat of them all was chronicled in the 2017 international publishing sensation, "Felix the Railway Cat," by English journalist Kate Moore. In this adorable tale (which we'd highly recommend), we learn how this kindly kitty in Yorkshire's Huddersfield station provided solace to lost children and brought a community together in the face of tragedy. We won't give away Felix's story as we wouldn't want to spoil your pleasure in reading it.

Finally, if you do fancy taking a tour around Britain with your cat, be aware that up to two "small domestic animals" can usually travel with their human for free. However, do check when buying your tickets that this marvelous "purr-k" still applies. There'd be nothing worse than your furry little darling seeming like a stowaway on the British rail system. Heaven forbid the very thought!

Feline-Friendly Lodgings

If you're planning to take your feline companion with you on a trip to the United Kingdom, the good news is that more than a few hotels welcome cats. Some of these British hotels even offer full-sized suites for cats. These accommodations have furniture, beds, and even televisions for the little critters. When it comes to food, the hotels provide an extensive menu, including everything from crabs to prawns, cod, and salmon, truly a feast to satisfy even the finickiest of felines. Cat owners can enjoy their vacations while the hotels take care of their pampered pussies in style.

The Meadow Cat Hotel in Cornwall is a famous luxury hotel for cats. The rooms provide reassurance and optimum comfort for the cats, with meadow-fresh air piped throughout. The hostelry offers bubble play sessions, relaxing music, spa services, and much more. They even have heated floors so your kitty can soak up some warmth in the damp British climate.

The Hotel Cat in New Forest is another great option if you're searching for temporary luxury lodgings for your beloved darling. A "country club for kitties," Hotel Cat is a seven-suite property about half an hour drive from London. The hotel offers a wide range of amenities, including free Skype calls (if your cat gets lonely), in-room TVs, and constant cuddles.

While you take an amazing trip to your favorite destination around Britain, your cat could have a great time at the hotel. Depending on what your kitty likes best, each room has a theme, from the beach to the forest. Hotel Cat also provides fine dining options such as crab and prawn medley dishes to delight your discerning kitty-cat.

However, don't think that the concept of cat lodgings is a 21st-century innovation. As long ago as the 19th century, prominent philanthropist and cat lover, the Duchess of Bedford, set up two distinct sets of cat accommodations in London. The first was a homeless cat's shelter (significantly ahead of its time!), and the second was a temporary lodging house where owners could leave their cats while on holiday. Previously, some thoughtless people had let their cats roam wild while they were away, reasoning that as cats are predators, they could fend for themselves.

Finally, the most glamorous and unusual of British hotel

cats is not even a real kitty. London's terribly grand Savoy hotel has a black cat sculpture called Kasper, whom they trundle out to avoid having an unlucky thirteen diners at tables in their dining room. Sculptor Basil Ionides created this charming cat artifact for the hotel in 1926. The wooden kitty is adorned with a napkin and served every delicious course his human dinner companions receive. This black cat not only brings good luck to the table but has the good fortune to enjoy a luxury dining experience many of us (cats and humans) would love to have!

A BLACK-AND-WHITE BRITISHER.
(*Photo: A. Warschcawiki, St. Leonards-on-Sea.*)

Britain is blessed with more than a few of the most well-bred felines. Here are just a few of the more intriguing or *aristo-cat-ic* bloodlines you might encounter. A few rather distinctive cats of less haughty provenance get a look in as well.

British Shorthair

The British Shorthair comes in a variety of colors and patterns. It is thought that these cats migrated to Britain along with Roman soldiers more than two thousand years ago. They became quite popular in the 19th century, showing up at many of the cat shows that were new and fashionable events at the time. They even made their way into the famed Crystal Palace of London, where the 1851 Great Exhibition was held.

The variety of British shorthairs is vast, though the current taste favors the British blue (a smoky gray in color and sporting bright blue eyes). There are also black, white, and black-and-white varieties, as well as tabby-striped and spotted kinds. These kitties possess rather reserved personalities—like the stiff-upper-lipped Brits themselves—but become very loyal and loving pets over time. They are also considered highly intelligent, watching all that happens with wide eyes. British shorthairs have a soft meow rather than a loud yowl. Of course, as their adaptability has proven, they handle cold weather exceptionally well.

Devon Rex

This British cat breed is relatively small, with very close-cropped fur and rather large ears. Maybe they take after Prince Charles! These adorable ears usually boast lovely little tufts of fur at the tips. Devon Rexes have a distinctive wedge-shaped head with broad cheeks and a pointed nose. Their legs are longer in the back, with front legs that are a bit bowed and shorter—this gives them great spring to their leaps and lunges. They don't usually appreciate the cold because of their thin fur) but they are highly spirited and will even play in the snow when motivated.

Considered a highly intelligent breed, many cat fanciers have found them easy to train. They tend to be especially devoted to their owners, and their curiosity stands out even amongst cats. One enthusiast once apparently described the Devon Rex as "a monkey in a cat suit," playful and intelligent, with a penchant for climbing and other frolicking antics.

The Devon Rex breed was first identified in 1959 in the county of Devon by one Beryl Cox. Once thought to be related to the Cornish Rex, genetic testing found otherwise.

Devon itself is famed for its dairies and the production of rich Devon cream, greatly appreciated by humans in the form of dollops of cream on jam scones. Cats being what they are, we're sure the occasional Devon Rex kitty helped itself to an odd surreptitious morsel or two.

Cornish Rex

The Cornish Rex is distinct from the Devon Rex in many ways. Its coat is longer and wavier, for one, and it boasts a more button-like nose. Identified a few years earlier than the Devon Rex, the original Cornish Rex was born to a Cornwall barn cat. The owner of the first identified Cornish Rex kitten thinks that the unusually wavy coat and distinctive features resulted from spontaneous mutations in random breeding. Over the years, the Cornish Rex has diversified, now coming in various colors and patterns.

For centuries Cornwall was famous for its tin mining. That industry produced the Cornish pasty: a delicious little meat pie meant to be held in the hands. The pasty allowed the miners to eat a quick lunch while toiling underground—perhaps saving a morsel for a hungry kitty to nibble on later.

The Manx Cat

One can readily recognize this rascal because it lacks a tail—though its personality more than makes up for that missing appendage. Like the Devon Rex, the Manx cat has longer hind legs, giving it exceptional power for leaping and running. The breed hails from the Isle of Man, an island between England and Ireland. While the lack of a tail has spawned many fascinating stories about how this tail-less state arose, the deficiency actually results from a genetic irregularity that can sometimes cause spinal problems and other deformities.

According to one legend, the Manx was out mousing just before Noah's ark was about to set sail. The cat was so dedicated to his task that he stayed out until the rain started to pour. As the Manx kitty rushed to fill the last place on the ark, Noah slammed the door quickly against the rain, catching the unfortunate cat's tail in the door and severing it. Yet another local legend claims that Manx cats result from breeding between cats and rabbits—a fanciful tale to be sure!

The Manx cat has become a beloved emblem of the Isle of

Man and graces stamps and coins, as well as decorating marketing and tourism materials. This small island is located in the Irish Sea between England and Ireland and is famed for being a tax haven and home to rally car racing. At one point, the island residents worried that, even though the Manx was being bred and popularized throughout the world, they were losing their native population of the breed. Thus, a government-run cattery was established to ensure the Manx cats' survival on their native isle. The breeding operation opened as a public tourist display in the mid-1960s and can still be visited today.

Scotland and Its Cats

The Scots are a proud bunch with a distinguished heritage, as well as a host of distinctive customs and quirks. They have a reputation for being industrious, and some stereotypes suggest that the Scottish people are careful with their money. Still, when it comes to cats, the Scots are as fond of them as anybody else and aren't afraid to splash out on some cat toys—in tartan patterns, perhaps?.

Here is some Scottish lore surrounding the magnificent feline:

— A mystical apparition that once roamed the highlands was known as a Grimalkin (from its gray color and the word "malkin," an archaic term for cat). The creature could take a human form during the daytime while assuming the guise of a fierce panther-like beast at night. Unsurprisingly, these mythical beings were linked to witchcraft and thought to be loyal minions of their witch mistresses and servants of Satan by extension.

— A particularly bizarre Scottish superstition regarding cats holds that if a woman eats food that a male cat has leaped over, she will become pregnant with kittens! A slightly less odd folk belief is that if you find a black cat on your porch, you will soon find prosperity, surely something particularly alluring to the Scots and their legendary financial cautiousness.

— Legend has it that the mouser at the oldest distillery in Scotland, Glenturret distillery, lived to hunt for nearly 24 years in the nineteen sixties, seventies, and eighties. Allegedly, he killed about 30,000 mice during his long reign, which earned him a spot in the *Guinness Book of World Records*. Towser, as this legendary mouser was called, apparently owed his long life to breathing in the fumes of the whisky—or "water of life"—at the distillery.

– A Scottish clan, Clan Chattan, uses a cat as its symbol: they are known as Mohr au Chat (basically, Great Wild Cat), and their motto is "touch not the cat without the glove." With that in mind, it might be best not to rouse the ire of any of the clan, also known as the Macphersons.

– Clan Farquharson, another offshoot of Clan Chattan, also boasts a coat of arms with two cats, demi-lions or Scottish wild cats, ready to battle.

Scottish Fold

This cat, named so for its ears that curl tightly over its head, appears to have been a spontaneous mutation. It dates back to the early 1960s. The matriarch of the breed was Susie, whose parents were ordinary farm cats with simple, straight ears. Susie's looks were so adorable, with her folded ears and big round eyes, that a local shepherd offered to breed any of her kittens who inherited her trait of distinctively crimped ears. Thus, human intervention initiated a line of cats with folded ears, usually with short hair and large expressive eyes. The long-haired version of the cat is known as the Highland Fold or Coupari cat (this version of its name pays tribute to the town of Coupar Angus, where the breed originated). They are even-tempered cats who can be playful.

Scottish Folds were accepted as a recognized breed by the late 1970s. They were bred with American shorthair cats, as well as British, to prevent any inbred genetic or developmental issues. Some Scottish folds have straight, perky ears, though these are barred from competitions. Some say the pretty pussycats resemble owls, as their small, forward-facing ears make their gorgeous eyes look even larger.

The Kellas Cat Hybrid

This intriguing kitty has relatively recent origins. In the 1980s, several reports coming from an area near the Eastern Scottish city of Inverness claimed that a long-legged black wild cat was living there. Specimens from the town of Kellas were caught and examined at the Natural History Museum, which eventually solved the mystery of their origins.

At first, people speculated that the Kellas cat may have been a newly discovered breed of wild cat or (less romantically) a domesticated black cat that had gone feral. Some suggested that it was a melanistic (or solid black) version of the already known Scottish wildcat, which usually looks like a tabby. It turns out that the Kellas cat is actually a hybrid of a domestic black cat, likely feral, and a Scottish wildcat. Still, the notion of some new, exotic wild cat captured the public imagination and provided much entertainment.

Wales and Its Curious Cats

The Welsh are known as feisty individuals, very independently minded, and distinct from the rest of the United Kingdom, even though England and Wales were unified in 1536. They have a dragon as a national symbol, so they're clearly not afraid of fearsome creatures and may even appreciate a certain wild streak in their pets. Wales was once the main center of coal production in the U.K., responsible for the blazing fires before which many a cat dozed. And, lest we forget, Wales was home to Howell Da, the ruler whose revolutionary laws regarding cats established a legal regard for feline well-being and value, all the way back in the 9th and 10th centuries.

The famous crooner Tom Jones comes from a long tradition of Welsh singers in chapel choirs. His famous version of

"What's New, Pussycat?" surely appeals to the feline crowd, and his seductive manner has made him famous with the ladies, a bit of a tomcat, you might say.

Another tasty treat of Welsh origin, the Welsh rarebit or Welsh rabbit, might, on the surface, seem appealing to your kitties. However, they'll be disappointed to know that it's simply a slice of bread covered in a cheese sauce and then broiled. There are many variants of the recipe's ingredients, but they can include Worcestershire sauce, pepper, flour, or even beer.

The Welsh are known to enjoy the camaraderie of their pubs. And, we shouldn't forget to tell you about the Welsh pub in Gwytherin that once boasted a lioness cub back in the 1970s. As a former patron succinctly said, "to see an actual lion at the Lion Inn was a big deal!" However, the big cat's stint at the pub only lasted a few months as she quickly became unruly and difficult to handle. We imagine she might be as tricky to deal with as some inebriated pub customers are at closing time!

The Welsh also have an astounding legend about a cat. We're referring to the tale of Cath Palug, perhaps the fiercest cat in mythological history. Born from the pig Henwen in the Welsh county of Gwynedd, the little cat was thrown into the sea but paddled away to the Welsh island of Anglesey. Once there, he grew up to cause all kinds of trouble, but this was not the usual sofa-clawing or blanket-tugging of a typical cat. The ferocious Cath Palug was responsible for the deaths of over 180 warriors before Sir Kay killed him. Other versions say the Cath Palug fought King Arthur, although it's unclear who won. We'd say that this particular feline might have been hard to place with a loving home!

There are a couple of fascinating Welsh superstitions that feature our feline friends. For example, they say it is bad luck to put a cat out before you wind the clock, which would have been done right before one went to bed. We suspect that some cunning cats might have come up with this superstition to allow them to spend more time indoors soaking up the warmth of the blazing Welsh coal fire! Women in Wales are also told to feed their cats well so that the sun will shine brightly on their wedding day. Who knows? If the sun shines on your nuptials, the cat gets the credit, and if it's a dreary day, your cat will probably say you didn't feed it quite enough!

HIGHER EDUCATION.

Newton's Necessity for a Cat Door

Born in Lincolnshire, England, during the late 17th century, Sir Isaac Newton was a skilled physicist, astronomer, mathematician, alchemist, and philosopher. As you'll remember from your schooldays, Newton defined the laws of motion and gravity, the theory of relativity. But– believe it or not– he may have invented the cat door!

According to Newton mythology, the scientist often conducted optical research in his dark laboratory. Now, Newton's cat Spithead had the awful habit of nudging himself through the door to the laboratory. This unwanted feline intrusion would let in light that would disrupt Newton's photosensitive experiments. And as Newton's third law states, every action has an equal and opposite reaction. So, Newton cut a small opening in the door covered by a dark black cloth to allow the cat to sneak in and out of his laboratory with minimal disturbance to the scientist. There you have it – the invention of the cat door!

Nowadays, some argue the claim to be fantasy, but it has been confirmed that there were indeed these small holes in the door of Newton's research room, and even one tiny aperture, sized for a kitten, maybe?

British Cats and Folk Medicine

Any discussion about the history of medicine must immediately acknowledge that there have been some strange ideas, wacky theories, and even zanier experiments. First, let's discuss a British folk cure for whooping cough in humans that might appeal to kitties as a special treat. We're speaking of none other than the British folk custom of feeding those humans afflicted by whooping cough with fried mice. Documented at least as far back as Elizabethan times, the rodent recipe was still recorded as a countryside cure in the 1920s. Although at that stage, whether fried rodents were still being consumed or whether the memory of this cure had been passed down through the generation is open to debate.

A published account from the 18th century establishes that a black cat could help cure eye problems. In the Reverend James Woodforde's *Diary of a Country Parson*, he suggests that rubbing a swollen eye with the tail of a black cat—no other color would do—would heal it right up. How did he know? Well, he took his black tomcat by the tail and rubbed his eye with it, reporting that "very soon after dinner, I found my Eyelid much abated of the swelling and almost free from pain." Or, could it have been some tankards of good old English ale that he consumed with his supper that dulled the pain? We'll let you be the judge...

Charles Darwin And Feline Humor

One of the most famous scientists in history, British naturalist, explorer, and founding thinker of the theory of evolution, Charles Darwin had a cat-like level of curiosity. However, he didn't show much early promise. Darwin's father went on record to predict of the young lad, "you care for nothing but shooting, dogs, and rat-catching, and you will be a disgrace to yourself and all your family." Mmmm, the critical parent couldn't have been more wrong... As we now know, Darwin's historic voyage on the HMS Beagle led him to the Galapagos Islands, its intriguing wildlife, and the idea of evolution. Still, Darwin was also fascinated by the less exotic forms of life he regularly saw at home, including the cats he saw every day. Darwin's consideration for our animal friends was far ahead of his time, and he perceptively noted in a notebook, "animals whom we have made our slaves, we do not like to consider our equal."

In *The Expression of Emotions in Man and Animals*, Darwin expanded on his theory of evolution. He argued that animals did, indeed, express emotions, and he contemplated the behavior of cats at one point. He noted that a cat's mood is expressed through its posture and movement—how it walks, how it flicks its tail, how it rubs up against people— and these displays reveal the cat's attitude. He observed that happy cats roll about on the floor or chase their tail and play. Darwin also noted that cats smile less than dogs, perhaps because "their more subtle and subdued humor seldom necessitates laughter."

It's incredible how it sometimes takes learned scientists quite a while to figure out what we lesser mortals might instinctively know.

Florence Nightingale

One of the most outstanding female figures in the history of medicine, Nightingale is recognized as the founder of modern nursing. The British woman was a great reformer of what were then abysmal patient conditions and worked diligently to streamline procedures and introduce hygiene in hospital settings. She was also a great lover of cats. There is no shortage of ink-smeared paw prints on many of her official papers!

Nightingale had at least 60 cats during her lifetime, up to 17 at one time. She claimed that "cats possess more sympathy and feeling than human beings," which is surprising for someone who provided such empathetic care to so many humans through her work. Nightingale believed that "a small pet animal is often an excellent companion for the sick, for long chronic cases especially." We'd say she probably had cats in mind when she said this. The medical pioneer was partial to Persians and named them for prominent figures of the day, such as Disraeli and Gladstone (after those two notable English Prime Ministers) and Bismarck (after the German statesman). Let it not be said that she wasn't international in her outlook! One might suggest that many future Persians should be blessed with their own dignified moniker of "Nightingale." We're sure the pioneering medical figure would approve!

World War I: Cats in the Trenches

Known as "the war to end all wars" (would that it had been so), World War I was devastating for Britain. It was the first conflict fought with aircraft, tanks, and other weapons of modern mass warfare. The experience of those in the trenches was quite brutal. The kingdom lost three-quarters of a million soldiers during the war, second only to Russia in terms of lives lost. Furthermore, many warriors came back seriously wounded, either physically or psychologically (or both).

During World War I, it is estimated that around half a million (!) cats were sent to the front lines. Of course, the troops prized the cats' abilities as mousers, but the kitties were also used to detect gas leaks and other hazards. Some felines even traveled by new-fangled airplanes, and many were lucky mascots for various units. It was also certainly the case that these brave and hearty felines comforted many a soldier on a cold winter's night or an ominous spring morning. There are numerous photographs (including photo postcards) documenting the soldiers' fondness for these cats and there are an abundance of accounts of the military rescuing kittens from battlefields and bombed sites.

World War II: Cat Heroes at Home

World War II, coming just a little more than two decades after the first global war, also brought tales of heroism and horror, complete with stories of true-blue kitty-cat companions and lucky feline mascots. During the war, Britain (especially London) was repeatedly bombed by the Germans, reducing whole areas to rubble and terrifying—and killing—many citizens and their pets.

Remarkably, dozens of cat owners in London credited their cats for *saving their lives*. Because cats have more sensitive hearing and are more attuned to vibrations, they would display signs of agitation or seek a safe place to hide *before* the air raid sirens even went off, alerting their owners about the oncoming bomber planes in the area.

In the book, *A Passion for Cats*, much-loved British actress Beryl Reid even claimed that her cat could distinguish between friendly English aircraft and hostile German bombers. The kitty would hide as the Nazi bombers swooped in but would stay put if English aircraft passed by. The British government acknowledged this feline ability by awarding many cats with medals that stated, "We Also Served." Any self-possessed British pussy cat would undoubtedly preen with pride at such an honor.

Cats were also employed to keep food supplies clear of rodents and other vermin—a duty they had always performed. This pest-fighting ability became especially important during the lean times of World War II. Cats patrolled the many Victory Gardens planted by British citizens to round out their meager rations, keeping the gardens free of pests. As we all know, cats are beneficial in times of trouble. The Brish certainly were glad of their support—and their companionship curing World War II.

An Overview

The significance of felines to English literary history cannot be overstated. Besides the famous Cheshire Cat with his elusive grin and Beatrix Potter's menagerie of beloved animals, one of the first pieces of literature written in English prose—instead of being translated from Latin or adapted from another language—is *Beware the Cat* by William Baldwin. Published in 1570, *Beware the Cat* reads more like a fairy tale or legend, starring the monstrous "Grimalkin," an enormous cat with an appetite to match, held in high esteem by the other kitties.

Baldwin's purpose here is satire. He compares the ravenous cat to the Pope in Rome, implying that the Pope—and

Catholicism by extension—should be considered greedy and even unholy. This satire caused a delay in the publication of the work, as Queen Mary, a devout Roman Catholic, was on the throne when the book was completed. The book was finally published once the Protestant Elizabeth I was crowned queen.

Chaucer's Cat-er-bury Tails

You may remember Geoffrey Chaucer's *The Canterbury Tales* from your school days. It remains a central text more than 600 years after its first publication—and it mentions kitties quite a few times! Chaucer was one of the first prominent authors to write in everyday English rather than in Latin (as was typical for the time).

If you want to experience *The Canterbury Tales* as early readers or listeners would, speak it with a thick Scottish accent, changing the vowels as you do so. You see, "meat" rhymed with "sweat" in the English of Chaucer's day. The pronunciation of "cat," however, stayed stubbornly the same, as cats themselves are wont to do.

Chaucer's love of cats is particularly evident when describing their beauty, and he seems especially taken with the sleekness and softness of their fur. In "The Manciple's Tale," the speaker offers advice on how to care for a cat, including feeding him "wel with milk" and providing him with a "couche of silk." Oh, yes, how today's kitties would approve of such luxurious spots to lounge upon. Things haven't changed at all since Chaucer's day in that regard! The writer also notes that a cat, no matter how well you ply him with milk or pamper him with silk, will drop everything to engage in hunting and eating a mouse.

Chaucer also mentions a cat in the Prologue to "The Wife of Bath's Tale." He explains how, if the kitty's tail gets burnt in the fire, she will mope about indoors. However, once "grown sleek" again, she will "sport with her tail and wonton in the sun." The mischievousness of the cat is meant to echo the friskiness of the Wife of Bath, whose vain, disobedient, and playfully lusty ways are legendary. Indeed, Chaucer often associates cats with sexuality. In "The Miller's Tale," the foolish Absalom would chase the lovely (but married) Allison like a cat chases a mouse: "I dar wel seyn, if she had been a mous, / And he a cat, he wolde hir hente anon" (he would have seized her right away). If you've not yet enjoyed Chaucer's bawdy tales, indulge your inner cat and pounce on them with gusto!

To Meow or Not to Meow?

Of course, William Shakespeare is considered the most influential figure in English literature. Not only did he change the course of English literary history, but he also changed the very language itself. He coined turns of phrase and memorable quotations on a scale unlike any other English author. His plays contain no shortage of allusions to cats. However, his attitude toward the furry feline could be rather negative, in keeping with the ideas about cats prevalent at the time.

Cats in Shakespeare's day were regarded with suspicion because of their alleged connection to witches, not to mention an association with disease. Nevertheless, Shakespeare did acknowledge cats' single-minded determination. For example, in *Henry IV*, Falstaff assures the young prince that he can trust him, for "I am as vigilant as a cat to steal cream." In other words, he is ready to assist Prince Henry in his designs for the crown, just as a cat would be eager to pounce on some delicious dairy products.

In several of his plays, Shakespeare uses the metaphor of cat-and-mouse to make his point. In *Pericles, Prince of*

Tyre, the cat is appreciated for his patience and hunting prowess: "The cat, with eye of burning coal, Now crouches fore the mouse's hole." Shakespeare also notes that, without the cat, the mice will play. In *Henry V*, Ely compares Scotland to the mouse when England (the cat) defends itself elsewhere: "Playing the mouse in absence of the cat, To tear and havoc more than she can eat." England must be ever vigilant, like the cat, in order to keep the wily Scots at bay.

Still, Shakespeare wasn't immune to the negative kitty propaganda of the day. His great rogue, Benedick, upon swearing that he will never allow himself to fall for a woman, claims, "If I do, hang me in a bottle like a cat and shoot me," implying that such a terrible fate would be routine (and acceptable) for a cat.

Dr. Johnson's "Very Fine" Feline

Commonly known as "Dr. Johnson," even though he never obtained a doctorate, Samuel Johnson's impact on English language and literature rivals Shakespeare's. For much of the eighteenth century, Johnson reigned supreme in the world of letters. His famed *Dictionary of the English Language* was nothing short of revolutionary for its time and has been described as one of the most erudite (not to mention charming) scholarly works ever produced. In addition to his prodigious efforts related to language, literature, and culture, as a poet, dramatist, essayist, and editor. Johnson was quite the cat lover.

Johnson's relationship with his beloved pet cat, Hodge, was detailed in John Boswell's superb biography, *Life of Johnson*. Johnson considered Hodge a kindred spirit, feeding him oysters and other delicacies. Indeed, there is even a statue of the esteemed Hodge outside Number 17 Gough Square in London, where he lived with his master for many good years

The statue shows the cat sitting on top of a dictionary, surrounded by empty oyster shells. Johnson himself purchased the oysters, "lest the servants having that trouble should take a dislike to the poor creature." The biographer Boswell recorded that Hodge could soothe the often-gruff Johnson. Boswell wrote that he had "frequently seen the ruggedness of Dr. Johnson softened to smiles, and caresses; by the inarticulate, yet pathetic expressions of his favorite Hodge." Like many of us incorrigible cat lovers, Johnson was convinced that ol' Hodge could understand him implicitly. He once commented that he had, perhaps, had better cats than Hodge. Still, upon glancing at Hodge's inscrutable expression, he quickly amended his statement, saying, "but he is a very fine cat, a very fine cat indeed."

Keats' Tribute to a Tomcat

The tragically short life of the Romantic poet John Keats did not impede his literary impact or output. Although he started off studying medicine, he quickly discovered his affinity for poetry—not to mention cats—at a relatively young age. Before he died of tuberculosis at the tender age of 26, Keats penned many notable poems, including "Ode to a Nightingale." However, he didn't confine his poetic tributes to animals to birds alone. I'm particularly fond of his tribute to a friend's old tomcat whose prime hunting days may have been behind him but whose claws are still sharp as ever they were. That poem is called "To Mrs. Reynolds' Cat," and here is an excerpt:

"How many mice and rats hast in thy days Destroy'd? How many tit bits stolen? - but pr'ythee do not stick Thy latent talons in me."

Dickens and his Furry Desk Mates

The most popular English writer of the 19th century, Charles Dickens produced numerous colorful novels, including *A Tale of Two Cities*, *Great Expectations*, and *Bleak House*, in which Lady Jane the cat plays a significant role. While Lady Jane, beloved by the sinister Krook, symbolizes the predatory nature of industrial England at the time, Dickens himself was quite the avid cat lover.

One of his cats gave birth in his study, and though Dickens was determined not to keep any of the kittens, he relented when one caught his fancy. Oh, how enchanting a cat's spell can be! The kitty was named 'Master's Cat' and became Dickens' frequent companion at his writing desk. When the kitty wanted her master's attention, she would extinguish his candle with a flick of her tail. Nonetheless, he greatly appreciated her presence, as indicated by his famous quote, "what greater gift than the love of a cat?"

A great chronicler of, and champion for, Britain's impoverished, it is perhaps no surprise that Dickens had such affection for cats as kitties would have been part of his early life when the expensive pursuit of keeping dogs or horses would have been beyond his family's reach. As the Victorian social reformer George Sims put it in his widely-read "How the Poor Live," cats were the natural companions of slum dwellers and were as common in poorer districts as "blackberries in September." This was presumably because cats required little attention while the working classes were away eking out a living and could survive by scavenging when times were tough.

The Brontës and Their Moggiës

The Brontës are arguably the most important family in English literature. Unfortunately, any attempt to chronicle the literary achievements of the sisters who produced *Jane Eyre, Wuthering Heights* and *The Tenant of Wildfell Hall* is far beyond the space I have available in this book or my meager skills as a literary commentator. However, suffice it to say that these ladies left a gigantic literary legacy. Having lost their mother and two older sisters at an early age, the siblings Charlotte, Emily, Anne, and their brother Branwell lived their formative years in a close-knit and somewhat isolated setting in a Yorkshire parsonage. Their first attempts at literature were minuscule books bound by hand-stitching and filled with tiny handwriting. These miniature publications were designed for the reading pleasure of their brother Branwell's little toy soldiers. Maybe the kitties who shared the Brontë home also had a furtive glance through the small-scale library!

The sisters were unabashed cat lovers with frequent references to their pets in poems and diaries. At the start of an essay, *The Cat*, penned in 1842, Emily wrote: "I can say with sincerity that I like cats; also I can give very good reason why those who despise them are wrong." Way to go, Emily!

The protagonist of Anne Brontë's novel Agnes Grey mentions that she "kissed the cat" when taking leave of her family and then burst into tears. However, it wasn't just their literary works that featured pussycats; several real-life furry friends graced the Brontes' home through the years.

Perhaps the feline king of the parsonage was Tiger, who was featured in a watercolor drawing by Emily and was said to have distracted her by swatting at her feet as she wrote *Wuthering Heights*. When Charlotte spent time at a school far away in Belgium, she wrote to say that she yearned to be at home as she would "save the best pieces of the leg of mutton for Tiger...[who] would be jumping about the dish and carving knife."

Another beloved Brontë moggy was the simply-named Tom. This handsome black cat was referred to in an 1833 report by a visitor to the Brontë household as "everybody's favourite." The connection of the Brontës to the feline world continues in modern times. During the coronavirus pandemic, the Brontë Parsonage Museum suffered a significant loss in revenue. However, this vital shrine to the Brontës was saved by a donation from the estate of T.S. Eliot, which offered it funding from income earned by the musical "Cats!"

Another reported modern feline link to the Brontë's home is that of a handsome black, long-haired feral cat who wanders around the graveyard near the church where the Brontës are interred. Quite a few visitors have noted his brooding, surreptitious presence. Some have taken to calling him Heathcliff and say his wild spirit can't be tamed...

The Real Cheshire Cat?

In *Alice's Adventures in Wonderland,* Lewis Carroll created perhaps the most famous cat in the history of British literature. The Cheshire Cat, with its infuriating grin and interminable riddles, still captures our imagination. However, the strange feline didn't spring fully formed from Carroll's imagination but was based on some existing British cat folklore. There are various explanations given as to the origin of the Cheshire Cat. Cheshire is a dairy district in England, famous for its cheese and other dairy products, and some folklore contends that a "Cheshire Cat" is one who would grin from ear to ear at the thought of so much yummy cream! Brewer's Dictionary of 1870 tells us that "cheese was formerly sold in Cheshire molded like a cat that looked as though it was grinning." The cheese would be cut into pieces starting from the tail end so that the last part remaining was the head of a grinning cat!

While the Cheshire Cat mocks Alice and can be a bit threatening, other evidence suggests that Carroll was quite fond of cats. As Alice falls down the rabbit hole at the beginning, she worries aloud about who will take care of her pussycat, Dinah. Dinah's kittens, Snowdrop and Kitty, also feature in the novel as lovable, cuddly imps. Carroll was known to take in strays on occasion. He allegedly once claimed to have given his cats "rat-tail jelly and buttered mice" for their morning meal. This anecdote was not too far-fetched for the author, whose work features walruses and carpenters feasting on oysters, not to mention dormice nesting in teapots!

Beatrix Potter's Menagerie

The beloved Beatrix Potter wrote and illustrated many fanciful children's books, replete with talking animals that are fashionably dressed. Her most famous work, perhaps, is *The Tale of Peter Rabbit*. 1907's *The Tale of Tom Kitten* was another favorite. This story warns of the futility of taming the rambunctious young felines, something many of us cat lovers can ruefully bear testimony to.

Tom's mother, Mrs. Tabitha Twitchit, wants to host an elegant tea party, so she proceeds to carefully groom Tom and his sisters, Moppet and Mittens. Tom scratches at her while she tries to groom him and is generally badly behaved. The kittens all go outside to play, dirtying their lovely clothes, and Tom bursts his buttons. It's implied that the jolly little kitty is a bit of a fat cat.

When they return home, their mother banishes the kittens to their rooms, telling her guests her children are ill. However, their boisterous behavior upstairs alerts the guests to their rambunctious wellbeing, and their mother's attempts to have a dignified gathering are thwarted. One cannot tame the wild spirit of a mischievous boy cat. It seems boys will be boys, whether human or feline.

The Cat Who Spoke English

Kingsley Amis was a renowned English writer of the 20th century, famous for such works as *Lucky Jim* and *The Old Devils*. Amis preferred the company of cats to that of humans: He stated, "I am enough of a cat lover to be suspicious of a household that doesn't have a cat... I associate a person having a cat with them being gentler than other people. Cats stimulate the fancy; we weave fantasies around them." The author also said of his own cats, "I love [them] because I love my home, and after a while, they become its visible soul." I feel Amis is on to something here, as almost every cat owner I know is also somewhat of a homebody and would agree that cats give any space a homey ambiance.

One of Amis's last cats, Sarah Snow, inspired him to write a poem in her honor, "Cat English." Here is a quick sampling of this ode to his cat's attempts to speak to him.

So when I came downstairs today

I was impressed to hear her say

"Hallo," Not like a person, true;

It might not sound quite right to you,

More of a simple squeak or squawk,

Still, that's what happens when cats talk."

Harry Potter's Quirky Cats

Some of the most successful books in modern history—J.K. Rowling's seven *Harry Potter* titles—feature cats prominently. This is evident from the first chapter of the first book, *Harry Potter and the Sorcerer's Stone*. We see Professor McGonagall watching Number 5 Privet Drive in her Animagus guise as a tabby cat. Rowling's cats often drive the plot or provide punch to pivotal scenes. Their presence in her books only highlights the continued association between feline familiars and their witchy (or wizard-y) companions.

The infamous Mrs. Norris, with her lamplight eyes and twitching tail, seeks out Harry, Ron, and Hermione as they sneak about the castle. Mrs. Norris plays an essential role in the second book, *Harry Potter and the Chamber of Secrets,* when she is petrified by the heir of Slytherin, which turns out to be a monstrous Basilisk.

In contrast, Hermione's bushy-tailed cat, Crookshanks, has an uncanny intelligence. While the cat annoys Ron with his antics against his pet rat Scabbers, clever Crookshanks is aware that the rat is a human masquerading as a rat. Indeed, Peter Wormtail is a criminal in hiding. Though Mrs. Norris and Crookshanks might have very different motives and trustworthiness, they both display typically feline traits of cleverness and curiosity.

Felines In the Visual Arts

Cats are regal enough to be featured in any number of paintings and other artworks by significant British artists. The great Thomas Gainsborough of "The Blue Boy" fame was an enthusiastic painter of cats. In an intriguing portrait of his daughters, "The Artist's Daughters with a Cat," the girls are accompanied by the family cat, who (perhaps resisting being forcefully cuddled) is biting one daughter's arm. The cat is barely visible and seems to blend in with the colors of the daughters' dresses. Maybe this implies that the kitty is such an integral part of the family that he cannot be distinguished from his humans?

130

One lesser-known but still highly-regarded artist specializing in cats is Bessie Bamber from Birkenhead (try saying that twenty times in a row!). Her works appeared at the very beginning of the 20th century, mainly featuring playful kittens. She primarily painted on porcelain and opaline glass, although she did complete one magnificent cat-themed mahogany panel. Her works bear titles such as "Two Kittens and Spilled Ink." She has a small but enthusiastic following, and her works fetch thousands of pounds at auctions.

In more recent years, famed British pop artist David Hockney created *Mrs. Clark and Percy* in 1970. The work portrays fashion designer Ossie Clark, his wife Celia Birtwell, and their white cat Percy. Mr. and Mrs. Clark face the artist, presumably honored to be depicted by the Pop-Art great. Meanwhile, the enigmatic feline turns his back to us and gazes out the window. Oh, trust a cat not to care about being painted by an artist whose most well-known piece, *Portrait of an Artist (Pool with Two Figures),* sold at auction in 2018 for a record-breaking $90 million!

English cats in three-dimensional form are also popular in British art. Many were mass-produced as smaller pottery ornaments, suitable for display on a mantelpiece or in a china cabinet. Such figurines include the Chelsea cats made throughout the 18th century and the later Derby, Rockingham, and Staffordshire cats. These became popular at around the same time that the rising middle class started to acquire a higher standard of living. This meant that luxury trinkets, such as these porcelain feline figurines, as well as food and care for pets like domestic cats, were now within their reach. So, just as real live cats were making their leap from mere rodent catchers to pampered companions, their porcelain representation also found a special place in British homes.

There are also quite a few larger-than-life cat sculptures dotted around Britain in various public places. There are two outdoor statues of Dick Whittington's cat in London, one in Highgate Hill and another in front of the Guildhall Art Gallery. The Heals department store features a bronze statue of a cat by a French sculptor that has a special spot on a back stairway where shoppers admire him on their way in and out of the store.

The store owner bought the sculpted kitty in 1905 as merchandise to sell in the store, but he came to like it so much that he decided not to sell it and gave it a permanent home in the store. Ah, well! Just another cat who insinuated himself into a loving home. The same old story...

There are many other examples of the feline presence in British art collections. For example, the Gayer-Anderson cat is a famous Egyptian sculpture of the cat goddess, Bastet, brought to England in the early 20th century and donated to the British Museum in 1939 by Major Robert Grenville Gayer-Anderson, of course.

Louis Wain and His Cats

Louis Wain's illustrations created an entire world of cats dressed as humans. Wain began drawing cats in earnest as his wife was dying. To comfort her. he drew pictures of her beloved cat, Peter. After her unfortunate and untimely death, Wain continued to produce sketches and illustrations of cats. The artist drew them participating in activities such as dining in cafes and playing musical instruments.

Wain's first published work, "A Kittens' Christmas Party," from 1886, is typical of his signature style, in which, as he put it himself, he set out "to wipe out the contempt in which the cat has been held." Wain's devotion to cats was legendary. He wrote a landmark 1889 book called "Our Cats and All About Them," His Who's Who entry states under the section for recreations, "no games of any sort at any time." Presumably, his love of felinekind was all-consuming.

Wain went on to design the official badge of the British National Cat Club, and many suggest that he is the most famous feline artist of all time. No less illustrious a figure than writer H.G. Wells of science fiction fame commented about Wain's fun and fabulous art: "He invented a cat style, a cat society, a whole cat world. English cats that do not look and live like Louis Wain's cats are ashamed of themselves." Indeed, Wain's cats represented the British gentlemen of the Victorian era, in all their civilized activities, including attending the opera, smoking, and playing cards. In his personal life, Wain was said to enjoy strolls along the beach with several cats in tow.

Wain's life had a disproportionate share of tragedy. Financially naïve, he didn't retain the rights to his drawings, and even though his work became wildly popular, he constantly had to produce new drawings to support himself. In 1914 he got badly concussed after being thrown from a horse-drawn bus. He was never the same, and his mental health steadily declined. Wain became violent and attacked his sister.

By 1925 the artist had ended up in the pauper's ward of the Middlesex County Mental Asylum. People hadn't forgotten him and his cat drawings were still much-loved. A visitor to the asylum noticed a quiet man in a corner "drawing cats" and realized that it was Wain. Soon, the Prime Minister became aware of the situation and had the artist transferred to what we hope were more pleasant surroundings at the Bethlehem Royal Hospital.

Throughout Wain's psychological struggles, he continued to draw cats, and we hope this brought him some relief. He certainly was ahead of his time, and the cat drawings of his very last years were of vivid, intense color. These works featured abstract patterns foreshadowing the psychedelic art of the 1960s. If you'd like to learn about this remarkable figure, Wain's life is the subject of a 2021film titled "The Electrical Life of Louis Wain," starring the prominent British actors Benedict Cumberbatch and Claire Foy.

Feline Museum Guards

There are displays of artfully arranged or painted cats in British art collections, but there are also real pussycats who patrol the corridors of some of the most venerable museums in Britain. For example, in the 19th century, the world-famous British Museum was home to Black Jack, a memorable feline resident of the Reading Room. Patrons were understandably taken with the genial fellow.

However, one night Black Jack was accidentally locked in a room containing some volumes of important newspapers. Distressed at being imprisoned, Black Jack shredded some of the spines and became, for a while anyhow, *purr-sona non grata*. Eventually, the kitty was admitted back to the museum, much to the delight of the patrons who had missed his company. Ah, yes, even the naughtiest kitties are usually forgiven their mischievous misdeeds.

Black Jack wasn't the only cat to make his mark on the British Museum., From 1909 to 1929, the institution housed a kitty named Mike. This feline would often bring a pigeon into the museum, which would be rescued while Mike was distracted with a less gory treat. Wallis Budge, Egyptologist (and Keeper of the Mummified Cats), made sure that Mike was properly fed even during the difficult years of World War I.

Mr. Budge grew to know his charge's tastes very well indeed, noting that Mike "preferred sole to whiting, and whiting to haddock, and sardines to herring; for cod, he had no use whatsoever." The finicky feline was beloved and was the subject of a 165-page obituary upon his passing. Museum officials even penned a poem for the occasion, which read, in part, "Old Mike! Farewell! We all regret you / Although you would not let us pet you, of cats, the wisest, oldest, best cat. / This is your motto—Requiescat."

Glasgow's Cat Curator

Smudge, another cat celebrity of the museum world, took up residence at the People's Palace Museum in Glasgow back in 1979. She was hired to take care of a bothersome rodent problem, and by all accounts, she executed her duties with great success. Her renown became so great that the museum began selling Smudge-adorned merchandise, including ceramic replicas of the black-and-white pussycat. The kitty was even voted in as a member of the General, Municipal and Boilermakers Trade Union. During a strike in the late 1980s, Smudge made an appearance on the picket line. She eventually retired from active duty in 1991 and died in 2000, at the very impressive age of 28.

Kippers Cat Meow-seum Shop

Purportedly the first dedicated cat museum in England, Kipper's Cats opened in 1989. It contains over 1000 items of fanciful feline-focused objects, from jewelry to plates to pictures and figurines. The location also hosts a pet shop with all sorts of pet supplies and accessories. The establishment's name comes from former owner Sylvia Taylor's one-time cat, Kipper, who resided in the pet shop cum museum his whole life. Here he watched over the cat-themed collection and commercial wares.

Since 2008, the meow-seum has been under the ownership of Catherine McCormick, and it aims to provide pet owners, particularly cat lovers, valuable advice about the care of their precious fur babies—and an opportunity to acquire some lovely cat-themed *objets d'art*.

What's in a Name?

Throughout their distinguished history, the British have come up with many fascinating and sometimes amusing names for their pampered pussycats. Here are the historical origins of some distinctive cat names:

– Before modern English, the nickname for a tomcat was a "gib" or "gibbe" cat: seemingly an abbreviation of the name "Gilbert." The term can be found both in Chaucer—in his translation of the *Romance of the Rose*—and in Shakespeare, where it is used more generally as a term for a broken down or worn-out animal.

– Modern British slang still uses the term "moggie" to describe a scruffy cat with affection. It once was employed to describe an older, disheveled woman ("moggie" is likely a corruption of "Maggie"). But, the word evolved into a description of a rather worn-down alley cat. As we all know, nowadays it's used affectionately for any ordinary cat.

– As of 2021, Glasgow's most popular cat name is "Loki," the character played by actor Tom Hiddleston in Marvel's cinematic franchise *The Avengers*. The people of Glasgow certainly admire the success of Hiddlestone, an actor from their hometown. And they are not alone! "Loki" is also one of the top most popular cat names in America.

– Americans have been inspired to name their cats after numerous other English royal figures such as "Diana," "William," "Harry," and "Elizabeth." According to the United States' veterinary hospital, Banfield, in 2017 the name "Diana" rose in popularity by 54%.

– A few other cherished cat names in the UK are "Missy," most commonly used in Leicester and Bristol, "Poppy" in Sheffield, and "Teddy" in Brighton and Hove. These names are common for people as well, with "Poppy" peaking as the fifth most popular name for girls in 2014. "Teddy" is often used as a name meaning "good" or "divine fortune."

Some British Cat Sayings

There are many sayings about cats that have an English provenance. Most of these were designed to teach folk wisdom and aimed to pass on (sometimes dubious) knowledge from one generation to the next. Here are some British cat-related sayings and their origins:

The old saying that a cat has nine lives was used in the late 16th century when it was featured in William Shakespeare's *Romeo and Juliet*. Juliet's cousin, Tybalt, inquired of one of Romeo's closest friends, Mercutio, "What wouldst thou have with me?" And Mercutio responded, "Good king of cats, nothing but one of your nine lives!"

While there are many unfortunate superstitions in the US concerning black cats, British black cats have been mainly associated with good luck. So, we have the intriguing proverb, "Whenever the cat of the house is black, the lasses of lovers will have no lack." We wonder how many lonely British ladies took this wisdom to heart and adopted black and kitties. We're also really curious to know if any handsome young lads showed up on their doorsteps afterwards.

In the midlands of England, black cats were a popular wedding gift to provide good fortune. In Yorkshire, fishermen believed they would obtain better yields with a black cat around. The belief was so widespread that fishermen would pay a high price for (or even cat-nap) these kitties to increase their fishing catches. In the 1600s, King Charles I of England was known to be closely attached to his black cat. One the day of his beloved cat's disappearance, King Charles said, "Alas, my luck has gone!" The next day, the royal was charged with treason and executed.

Another common English proverb is "The cat's out of the bag," which means that previously hidden truths have been revealed. The colloquial usage may have come from the "cat o'nine tails," a whip used as a brutal discipline in the Royal Navy. The whip was stored in a burgundy sack. So *the cat* would be *let out of a bag* to be used for punishment whenever a sailor's misdoings came to light.

And finally, there's the old saying about "putting a cat among the pigeons." The reserved English really don't like to do this because it would ruffle a bunch of feathers, something the generally low-key British are loathe to do. We should also note that pigeons are important to British culture: both as presences in very important public areas such as London's Trafalgar Square and as racing pigeons in people's homes mainly in the north of England. In many ways, both cats and pigeons are a central part of urban British life and we could not imagine life without either of them—even when the fur and the feathers fly.

A Cat's Home Is His Castle

Have you ever heard the phrase, "An Englishman's home is his castle?" Originating in the 17th century, and first articulated in a more complex form by the British legal scholar Sir Edward Coke, this saying set forth the principle that householders can use reasonable force to protect their property from thieves and trespassers. It emphasized that nobody could enter a man's house without express permission and due authorization. Thus an ordinary man could feel like an all-powerful lord of the manor, secure in his domain.

British cats were (and are) no less protective of their

abodes. One mother cat in London, in particular, was very passionate about the sanctity of her home. Her suburban home was sold, and her owner moved away, leaving her behind. For shame! Several days later, the new tenant tried to move in, only to be deterred by the defensive kitty. Hissing and snarling, the cat kept the new tenant captive for three hours before the fire department came to the rescue. Talk about protecting one's castle! Like the British, cats are particularly attached to locations they've become used to and can become disoriented when they have to move. Unlike perhaps in, let's say, the United States, where people may be more willing to move for career advancement or education, the Brits tend to want to stay put. And, on the subject of cats, castles, and protecting one's domain, one of the oddest feline-related pieces of art we have ever come across is a 17th-century British engraving depicting cat soldiers defending their castle from an invading rat army. "The Cats' Castle Besieged and Stormed by the Rats" is said by some to have a hidden political significance. However, most sources say that even if it originally had such a meaning, it was enjoyed by most who saw it as a delightful work of cat-themed fantasy...

It's hard for the modern mind to grasp, but British prints in the 16th through 19th centuries functioned somewhat like Internet memes. Such prints with comical or political sub-texts were printed cheaply and distributed in their thousands. People could gaze at the latest images in the windows of the printmakers and perhaps buy a copy to bring home and put on their wall. They were passed around among friends and acquaintances, sometimes even going what we might call "viral."

A Scrumptious Spread Indeed

Although sometimes maligned as being plain and stodgy, British food, in its better manifestations, is rather good, especially when it uses fresh ingredients that come directly from Britain's many small-scale traditional farms. What's more, British cooking is far less narrow in scope and insular than it is sometimes claimed to be. For instance, sausages were introduced to Britain by the Romans. Sugar, potatoes, and bananas came from the New World, and curry from India in the 18th and 19th centuries.

Long before American-style fast food became popular in Britain, an American businessman named James Spratt offered the British the first commercial cat food. His widely-sold "Spratt's Patent Cat Food" was advertised proudly as being filled with meat from American buffalo. However, many domestic cats in British cities in the 18th and 19th centuries would have been fed cheap (and often unsavory) cuts of meat sold by "cat's meat men." These merchants wandered the streets, calling out loudly to alert householders that they were in their neighborhood. We're sure the kitties in these areas perked up their ears with delight when they heard the cries of the "cat's meat men!" This source of cat food survived at least until the 1930s in the form of a Cat and Dog's Meat Shop on London's Bishop's Bridge Road.

In more recent years, British cats tend to dine on commercial pet food produced by large multinational manufacturers. However, as is the case anywhere else, British cats also wheedle tasty tidbits from their humans. In 2012, the British tabloid newspaper, *The Daily Mail*, shared details of a survey in which it was revealed that a staggering 45 percent of British cat owners share fish and chips with their pets about once a week. While takeaways in excess are bad for humans, they're even worse for our furry fuzzballs, leading to obesity and ill health. Cat owners of Britain, please keep the "chippy supper" on your plates out the reach of demanding paws. We all know how insistent cats can be in their pestering and pleading. Still, it's best to put on a British "stiff upper lip" and ignore them as best one can...

SANDY STEALING THE MILK.
THE PROPERTY OF MISS HARPER.
(*Photo: B. Tugwell, Haywards Heath.*)

A Cat's Dubious Moral Character

Cats may have the most morally ambiguous attitudes of all creatures, as evidenced by their lack of care about how their actions affect others. Even our favorite darling kitties are capable of criminal acts. More often than not, when disrespecting the rules, cats escape being called to account for their actions. This is, admittedly, a source of envy for many humans. Just imagine if you could lead such a consequence-free life! Oh, to live as a cat does…

20 - GOT TO PICK A POCKET OR TWO!

Cat Burglars

Criminality and society's reaction to it feature prominently in British history and literature. We've all heard of the poor desperate individuals sent to the New World for robbing something as insignificant as a handkerchief. I'm sure you've also come across Charles Dickens's much-loved novel, *Oliver*. Who can forget its lively descriptions of a band of juvenile thieves whom the evil Fagin trained to 'pick a pocket or two!"

Unlike Dickens's villain Fagin, Londoner Elaine Floodgate found herself with a nest full of cat thieves that she hadn't trained in their evil ways. She was horrified when her two precious pets began to burglarize the London suburb Elaine called home. Her neighbors had noticed items disappearing but couldn't identify the culprit. Certainly, Elaine didn't think much of the crime wave at first. Then she saw one of her cats, Major Benjie, with a stuffed boy animal that had been reported missing. The next theft was committed by her other cat Georgie, who made off with a significantly larger prize, an expensive watch. Elaine returned the items and saw to it that the cat burglars were barred from returning to the crime scene. There are no reports of whether the criminal kitties re-offended. We have our doubts...

Grave Robbers

Do you think your cat's a handful? Just imagine if you had to deal with the dastardly deeds of one very naughty British cat...

Cat owner Samantha Wilks of Teesside noticed her fur baby bringing home a suspicious amount of stuffed toy animals. At first, she assumed they were from her neighbors' homes until a newspaper reported vandals stealing stuffed toy animals from children's graves. After some investigation, Samantha's suspicions were confirmed. Her darling pet was caught lifting cuddly toys from a cemetery in Durham Road, Stockton. He had made off with over 50 toys! With his limited access to stores to obtain his own, kitty simply resorted to "borrowing" the little friends from the nearby cemetery. Perhaps Samantha bought her feline some cuddly friends of his own, so he wouldn't have to "borrow" others from elsewhere! Or, maybe she issued a stern reprimand. We're not sure whether either course of action might have been that effective. Like elsewhere, cats in Britain simply don't care too much when they break the rules of mere humans.

21 - Jolly Good Cat Sports!

These British Cats are "on the Ball!"

Soccer (or football as it's more commonly referred to in Britain) is the most popular British team sport to watch and participate in. It's widely held that the official history of modern-day soccer dates from the founding of The Football Association in 1863. However, this game has been played in a much broader and more-freewheeling form for centuries. "Ball," as it was more commonly known, extended over whole neighborhoods or country districts. The goals could be up to three miles apart!

The sport was rough and ready. The players' antics resembled those of marauding hellcats. Ball was immensely popular. Various English kings lamented that too many Englishmen were playing football instead of practicing archery. Apparently, this was weakening the nation's ability to protect itself from marauders. In more recent years, cats have featured in Britain's most loved game in several rather remarkable ways. London's now-demolished White City Stadium was home to some notable soccer games (including the legendary 1966 World Cup). Since its founding in 1908 as an Olympic stadium, White City was also home to the world's best rat-catching cat. This lovely tabby, who has unfortunately remained nameless, caught at the very least 12,480 rats in six years! Her daily average was almost seven rats a day. Whoah! That's quite a record.

Successful soccer players in Britain enjoy public adulation and financial remuneration most could only dream of. Many British kids dream of becoming a top soccer player. It's hardly a surprise then to learn that some British kitties also want to run about to the applause of a massive crowd of soccer fans.

In 2019 one particular black kitty took to the pitch in the

middle of a match between top teams Liverpool and Wolverhampton. Initially, it seemed that the furry wanna-be footballer would just take one run across the pitch. However, to the crowd's delight (and presumably to the players' annoyance), the kitty dashed back and forth with great agility and skill. She evaded all attempts to stop her. After three or four minutes of these antics, staff and police managed to get her off the pitch.

The feline football sensation was part of a colony of feral cats who inhabited the football ground and were fed by football fans. We hope that in future, the frisky kitty confines her sporting activities to watching from the stands. Or, based on her talent and speed, should the football club be trying to recruit and train her? Sign her up, we say!

Off to the Races!

Britain's second-most popular spectator sport (after soccer) is horse racing. Britons have been enjoying this pastime since Roman times. The sport contributes a billion pounds sterling (approximately $1.3 billion) to the British economy each year. Millions are wagered on every race. So, it's no wonder that everything possible is done to ensure the fitness and wellbeing of the specially bred and reared British racehorses. One interesting strategy to keep the priceless steeds in top form is to have special stable cats whose sole purpose is to calm the mighty beasts by living in the horses' stalls alongside them.

Legendary 18th-century British painter of horses Goerge Stubbs (whose equine portraits grace the Royal Collection of art) ensured that his depiction of the famous stallion Godolphin Arabian featured a cat. This particular kitty was none other than the horse's stable companion. When the prize horse died, his feline roommate stayed by the body and could not be budged until the mighty steed was buried.

Keeping stable cats with prize horses must have been pretty standard in Britain. In a story by P.G. Wodehouse, the plot features an attempt to kidnap a stable cat and thus distress the horse so much that it won't win a race that it otherwise would have been sure to win.

Speaking of cats and racing, would it surprise you to know that in the 1930s, there were reports of cat racing from the town of Portisham in Dorset? Well, we were intrigued to un- cover such accounts. The story was widely repeated in newspapers at the time. However, it was simply a hoax to garner publicity for the town. It also was presumably great fun for all those involved in the prank. The locals came together and invented details of cats chasing an electric mouse around a track. To add substance to the story, some stray cats were rounded up and photographed on a scales as if to imply that they were being weighed before the race.

A Huntin' We Will Go...

Hunting is one of those pursuits closely associated with the British upper classes. It conjures up images of gents in immaculately tailored tweeds. Of course, no English hunting scene would be complete without sporting dogs who will retrieve the prey once it's been shot. So, it was with great curiosity that I came across a blog post by the author Mimi Matthews on 'Sporting Cats in the 19th Century.' It seems there were some British newspaper accounts of people using cats as hunting retrievers. One particularly clever old man would shoot birds flying overhead who might then fall into his neighbor's property, on which it would be illegal to trespass. The wily fellow had trained his cat to creep undetected onto the neighbor's property and retrieve the fallen birds. We presume man and feline shared the catch. Otherwise, we're sure the kitty wouldn't have continued in the enterprise without his share of the feathered profits. We all know what cats are like!

22 - The Future for British Cats

Nearly a quarter of English adults own a cat. Projections estimate the British pussycat population will reach its highest number yet (over 12 million) in 2023. Despite Britain's aristocratic traditions, it's noteworthy that the plain old moggie rules the roost in Britain. Fewer than 10% of British pet cats are pedigree felines, unlike in the US, where about 40% are members of a registered breed.

Cats encompass both sides of the British character, standoffish at first and then becoming eccentrically exuberant upon closer acquaintance. Whether aristo-cat or commoner, cats and kittens of all ilks hold a special place on laps and by firesides across Britain. From barn cats to those who dwell in the grandest dwellings in the land, we're confident that the 'Cats of Britain' will continue to prosper. Therefore, we implore you, ladies and gents, young and old, to raise a glass of good, old-fashioned cheer to those cherished felines the British hold so dear!

Hip, hip hurrah! Three Cheers for the Cats of Britain!

23- SPECIAL BONUS!

Want This Bonus Book for FREE?

Get <u>FREE</u>, unlimited access to it and all of my new books.

subscribepage.io/h6Fz5k

24 – If you liked this book...

Purrr-leeze leave a review!

https://tinyurl.com/5tdxktyr

A cat fanatic and book lover, I write fascinating books about our beloved kitties and how they've shaped our world..--*If you love cats, you'll love my books*

-- **So, why not join my "Cats of the World" fan club? You can read all my new books FOR FREE?**

AND... You'll get a <u>free</u> bonus book, "British Cats in Show Biz...

SIMPLY SCAN THE CODE OR CLICK THE LINK TO JOIN! There's **no cost** to you

https://rb.gy/bp3aox

27 - Credits for Illustrations

Some Very British Concepts

1871, The First National Cat Show at the Crystal Palace —illustration from The Book of The Cat (1903), in the public domain
https://openlibrary.org/books/OL7205700M/The_book_o f_the_cat

Upper-Crust Kitties

illustration from The Book of The Cat (1903), in the public domain
https://openlibrary.org/books/OL7205700M/The_book_o f_the_cat

Cats Who Meant Business

Public domain -downloaded from https://picryl.com/media/marketing-by-louis-wain-064a50

A Long and Distinguished History

illustration from The Book of The Cat (1903), in the public domain

https://openlibrary.org/books/OL7205700M/The_book_o
f_the_cat

An Ever-Expanding Empire

Vintage advertising card, CCO Public Domain https://
www.publicdomainpictures.net/en/view-image.php?
image=280786&picture=cats-with-world-globe

Especially British Eccentrics and Their Cats

https://picryl.com/media/owl-and-cat-calligraphy-a5b67e.
In the public domain.

Travel and Tourism

illustration from The Book of The Cat (1903), in the public
domain
https://openlibrary.org/books/OL7205700M/The_book_o
f_the_cat

Felines and Scientific Progress

illustration from The Book of The Cat (1903), in the public domain
https://openlibrary.org/books/OL7205700M/The_book_o f_the_cat

Cats in Wartime Britain

https://poulwebb.blogspot.com/2017/01/louis-wain-part-7.html

The Artistic Side of British Cats

illustration from The Book of The Cat (1903), in the public domain
https://openlibrary.org/books/OL7205700M/The_book_o f_the_cat

Home Comforts

illustration from The Book of The Cat (1903), in the public domain
https://openlibrary.org/books/OL7205700M/The_book_o f_the_cat

Got to Pick a Pocket or Two!

illustration from The Book of The Cat (1903), in the public domain
https://openlibrary.org/books/OL7205700M/The_book_o f_the_cat

Jolly Good Cat Sports!

Louis Wain, Cats Playing Football http://www.artnet.com/artists/louis-wain/cats-playing-football-eIpYoq3vm5CC9RxNloEbmQ2. In the public domain.

The Future for British Cats

The Bachelor Party, Louis Wain, public domain, via Wikimedia Commons https://picryl.com/download-

Enjoyed this book? Please leave a review...

illustration from The Book of The Cat (1903), in the public domain
https://openlibrary.org/books/OL7205700M/The_book_o f_the_cat

About the Author

Photograph author's own--Free for commercial use, no attribution required

Enjoyed this book? Please leave a review...

illustration from The Book of The Cat (1903), in the public domain
https://openlibrary.org/books/OL7205700M/The_book_of_the_cat

Thank You

As we reach the end of this book, I want to say thanks for reading this book.

I want to get this information out to as many people as possible. If you found this book helpful, I would greatly appreciate you leaving me a review. This helps others find the book as well.

Disclaimer

This document is geared towards providing exact and reliable information in regards to the topic and issue covered. The author has done his best to be accurate and provide a balanced view of historical events and figures. I am not responsible for any errors contained in this book, or for any consequences thereof. This information is for entertainment purposes only.

The information provided herein is stated to be truthful and consistent, in that any liability, in terms of inattention or otherwise, by any usage or abuse of any policies, processes, or directions contained within is the solitary and utter responsibility of the recipient reader. Under no circumstances will any legal responsibility or blame be held against the publisher for any reparation, damages, or monetary loss due to the information herein, either directly or indirectly.

Last Updated: June 2022

Made in the USA
Columbia, SC
06 December 2022

72814568R00105